. . . . a scripture and prayer journal

Born to Soar

Unleashing God's Word in Your Life

melissa
overmyer

servant
AN IMPRINT OF
FRANCISCAN MEDIA
Cincinnati, Ohio

Published with ecclesiastical permission of the Archdiocese of Washington, DC.

This journal is a component of the Something Greater Ministries study series. For more information about the *Born to Soar* online study, go to www.FranciscanMedia.org. "Prayer to Care for Our Common Home" is reprinted with permission of the U.S. Conference of Catholic Bishops. All rights reserved. Selected quotes have been taken from *The Collected Works of St. John of the Cross*, translated by Kieran Kavanaugh and Otilio Rodriguez, copyright ©1964, 1979, 1991 by Washington Province of Discalced Carmelites. ICS Publications, 2131 Lincoln Road, N.E., Washington, DC 20002-1199, U.S.A. www.icspublications.org. Used by permission. Scripture passages have been taken from *New Revised Standard Version Bible*, copyright ©1989 by the Division of Christian Education of the National Council of the Churches of Christ in the U.S.A. Used by permission. All rights reserved.

Cover and book design by Mark Sullivan

LIBRARY OF CONGRESS CATALOGING-IN-PUBLICATION DATA

Names: Overmyer, Melissa, author.

Title: Born to soar : unleashing God's word in your life : a scripture and prayer journal / Melissa Overmyer.

Description: Cincinnati : Servant, 2017. | Includes bibliographical references and index.

Identifiers: LCCN 2017005765 | ISBN 9781632531735 (trade paper : alk. paper)

Subjects: LCSH: Spiritual journals—Authorship. | Diaries—Authorship—Religious aspects—Christianity. | Spiritual Life—Christianity. | Prayer—Christianity.

Classification: LCC BV4509.5 .O93 2017 | DDC 248.4—dc23

LC record available at https://lccn.loc.gov/2017005765

ISBN 978-1-63253-173-5

Published by Servant, an imprint of
Franciscan Media
28 W. Liberty St.
Cincinnati, OH 45202
www.FranciscanMedia.org

Printed in the United States of America.

I dedicate this book to my mother, Joan Pennington, who taught me how to pray and, by God's grace, enabled my soul to soar; to Fr. Zachary Dominguez and Fr. John Pietropaoli, who breathed wind under my wings; and to Maribeth Harper, who took this book from egg to imago.

In March 2013, shortly after his election, the Pope explained his reason for taking the name of Francis of Assisi: "Francis was a man of peace, a man of poverty, a man who loved and protected creation."

By God's grace, may this book be instrumental in helping you to experience deep and abiding peace that can only come through connection with God. And in studying the life of the monarch (*Danaus plexippus),* may you also have a heightened sense of appreciation for God's creative genius, expressed so beautifully in the prayer by the U.S. bishops in response to Pope Francis's apostolic exhortation, *Laudato Si: On Care for Our Common Home.*

• • •

PRAYER TO CARE FOR OUR COMMON HOME
Father of all,
Creator and ruler of the universe,
You entrusted your world to us as a gift.
Help us to care for it and all people,
That we may live in right relationship –
with You,
with ourselves,
with one another,
and with creation.

Christ our Lord,
both divine and human,

You lived among us and died for our sins.
Help us to imitate your love for the human family
by recognizing that we are all connected—
to our brothers and sisters around the world,
to those in poverty impacted by environmental devastation,
and to future generations.

Holy Spirit,
giver of wisdom and love,
You breathe life in us and guide us.
Help us to live according to your vision,
stirring into action the hearts of all—
individuals and families,
communities of faith,
and civil and political leaders.
Triune God, help us to hear the cry of those in poverty, and the cry of
the earth, so that we may together care for our common home.

Amen.

CONTENTS

You Were Created for Something Greater

Can you recall a time when you looked at your life and thought, "There must be something more than this"? Have you ever longed to experience something more? Something better? *Something greater?*

THE HUNGER OF THE SOUL

What is it that *you* want most in life? For most people, happiness is high on the list. I know it is high on *my* list! All I really want from life is peace, love, and joy—happiness—for everyone. You know, for life to "work," not only for myself but also for others. (And, if I am being really honest, I would also like a fabulous pair of shoes, preferably on sale.)

Over the years, I have tried different formulas for achieving this state of bliss, but again and again, I have had to face one important truth: Unless I am connected to God, who invented the happiness I'm seeking, I come up frustrated, angry, and disappointed by life—empty instead of full. When I feel disconnected from God, I feel restless—not at peace with myself, with my God, or with others.

Have you ever experienced this kind of restlessness, this kind of hunger for happiness?

If so, there is a reason for it: When he created us, God placed inside us the desire to know him and to be united to him. Just as we experience physical hunger pangs when we need to fuel our bodies, we experience spiritual hunger pangs—angst that nothing in this world can satisfy—when we need to fill our souls.

Sadly, our culture has done its very best to numb us to the ravenous cries of our souls, so much so that we may not even recognize that our longing for happiness is a spiritual longing. We look with envy at our neighbors and friends and think that we will find happiness if we just acquire…something more—a bigger house, a higher-paying job, better-behaved children, a more illustrious education, or a more attentive spouse—more, bigger, or better of just about anything. We keep looking for something that will satisfy this gnawing hunger. But try as we may, we cannot find the right something to satisfy us. It is as if our life is a puzzle and we have found all of the right pieces, save the one in the very center that makes the entire picture come together and work. We need something else, something greater than this world can provide.

Soul Food

The good news is that God the Father, in ancient Holy Scripture, promised us Something Greater: food for our souls that brings with it lasting peace, unconditional love, and unending joy that far exceed anything this world has to offer. And God kept his promise.

The Something Greater God promised turned out to be an encounter with God himself: the one, true, triune God is the food our souls crave. God was born into the world through Mary as God the Son, Jesus Christ; after Jesus died for us and returned to the Father, he left us the Eucharist and also sent God the Holy Spirit to remain with us always. And God does not want us just to know *about* him; he wants us to know him as we know our closest friends, to have an intimate union with him that will satisfy the longing of our hearts.

Are you ready to seek that close union with God and feel your heart filled and transformed by his grace?

One of the most important ways God makes himself known to each of us is through the Bible. The book we call the Bible is really a library of divinely inspired manuscripts covering the history of thousands of years of God's relationship with his people, all knit together by a single golden strand of truth that runs from beginning to end. In our study, we will use this holy text to lead us to the source of our much-longed-for "soul food"—our "bread from heaven" (Exodus 16:4; John 6:51) that satisfies the hunger of our souls.

The Bible is broken into different parts. We learn in the New Testament about the life, works, and effects of Jesus, the promised Messiah (savior) who was prophesied in the Hebrew Old Testament. The first four books of the New Testament, the Gospels (*Gospel* means "good news"), are histories of Jesus's life, teachings, death, and resurrection. The Gospels are named after the four men who wrote them: Matthew, Mark, Luke, and John.

In the Gospels, Jesus introduces us to God the Father and invites us into his heavenly realm right here on earth, the kingdom of God. He opens our eyes to see that there are two kingdoms: the kingdom of this world, which we can touch, taste, see, hear, and smell (our physical world), and God's kingdom, which is unseen but just as real—in fact, even more so.

By getting to know Jesus Christ and learning how to connect with him spiritually, we can become "kingdom-of-God dwellers." But because we have been given the gift of free will, each of us must decide, every minute of each day, in which kingdom we will choose to place our hope and trust. St. Paul, one of Jesus's most passionate followers, urges us to "set your minds on things that are above, not on things that are on earth" (Colossians 3:2).

When we learn to tap into God's kingdom, connect with God, and fill our hungry souls with him, the aching, longing, and emptiness are at last satisfied. The growling hunger is satiated, and life begins to work. When we open our hearts and say yes to God, asking him to reveal himself to us, Jesus always answers that prayer by pouring out his grace, making us stronger and more sensitive to his guiding presence.

Come, embark on a lifelong spiritual journey that will allow you to spread your wings and take you to the heart of Something Greater.

You will experience a true metamorphosis of your soul, a satisfying of your spiritual hunger. By learning about and experiencing friendship and union with Jesus Christ through prayer and meditation, receiving the sacraments, studying the Scriptures, and embracing the spirituality of the Catholic Church, you can at last be filled to overflowing. Come find out what the apostle John, the best friend and beloved disciple of Jesus, meant when he told the first Christians that "the one who is in you is greater than the one who is in the world" (1 John 4:4).

A Spiritual Metamorphosis

Born to Soar: Unleashing God's Word in Your Life was inspired by St. Paul's New Testament Letter to the Romans, which reads:

> Do not be conformed to this world, but be transformed by the renewing of your minds, so that you may discern what is the will of God—what is good and acceptable and perfect (Romans 12:2).

FOLLOWING THE MONARCH INTO FLIGHT

The Greek word for *transformed* is the root for the English word *metamorphosis*—a major change of form or shape. If we want to be truly like God, to be changed to resemble him, we must renew our minds to his truths. In this study we will look daily at God's truths found in his Word and, little by little, we will see our minds renewed by those truths. A renewed mind begets renewed thinking. Renewed thinking leads to a renewed heart. A renewed heart brings forth renewed actions. And renewed actions result in renewed lives. Big change is coming.

How will we seek, find, and absorb these life-transforming truths?

From the moment of our conception, God has desired to fill us with an understanding of his infinite and personal love for us. God reveals himself in countless ways to those who listen. Many times in Scripture, Jesus points to something very familiar in nature—wheat, lilies, fish, seeds—to help us grasp the depth of his unconditional love for us. In the book of Job, one of the oldest books of the Old Testament (Hebrew Scriptures), Job declares:

> But ask the animals, and they will teach you;
>   the birds of the air, and they will tell you;
> ask the plants of the earth, and they will teach you;
>   and the fish of the sea will declare to you.
> Who among all these does not know
>   that the hand of the LORD has done this? (Job 12:7–9)

Following Jesus's example and Job's directions, I am basing this six-week prayer, meditation, and Scripture study on the life cycle of the North American eastern migrating monarch butterfly—*Danaus plexippus.* The more I have studied and pondered these butterflies, the more I have come to see that their lives reveal a nearly perfect picture of God's providential plan for our spiritual growth, from birth in baptism to full maturity—and ultimately to eternal life.

Not only can this butterfly's life cycle teach us about the metamorphosis of our souls from baptism to eternal life, but it can help us to see how we grow spiritually each day, each moment, and to understand that we can be open to the transforming grace of the Master Creator of all, God our Maker.

It is profound to me that the life cycle of a butterfly can speak so clearly to us of God's love and revolutionary ways, and I hope to share my appreciation for the creative, even artistic, way our Lord designed these beautiful creatures! Of course, my deepest desire is that, as you ponder his written Word and learn to connect to him in prayer and meditation over these next six weeks, you will receive from God himself a revelation of his personal love for you.

God longs for us to know him. Come with me as we set out to see what spiritual lessons we can learn from one of the Creator's most exquisite and fascinating creations—the butterfly.

St. John of the Cross: Mystic, Poet, and Spiritual Guide

St. Teresa of Avila, a sixteenth-century Spanish Carmelite nun who was named the first female Doctor of the Church, wrote about the spiritual lessons that can be drawn from the silkworm in her spiritual classic *Interior Castle*. Those who have come to know and love her writings are often delighted to discover the mystical poetry of her prayer master, spiritual director, and beloved friend, the Carmelite friar and priest St. John of the Cross. St. John experienced many hardships and trials in his life, and his poetry often reflects his deep need to draw close to God in hard times.

Do you ever feel alone, tested, or misunderstood? Reading St. John's poetry reminds us to draw strength and peace from God whenever we need it.

I have chosen to introduce, in the simplest of ways, the poetry and ideas of St. John of the Cross into this study. We will in no way plumb the depths of his spirituality, but excerpts of his poetry are woven throughout the study. We will witness his passionate love for God and sample his exhortations on detachment, solitude, trust, patient endurance, humility, and love of nature. I pray that, as you reflect on his beautiful poetry, you will get a sense of the deeply loving and passionate relationship that St. John of the Cross had with God—the sort of relationship God longs to have with each of us.

Reading St. John's works, we will discover that prayer is not at all about learning a formula or memorizing words—it is, at its core, about falling in love with God and learning to soar upward, ascending to heaven.

Scope of This Study

This study is intended for those who are fairly new to Scripture study and are simply looking to connect with God in a meaningful, personal way. After working your way through this journal (with or without the video series, also available through Franciscan Media), you will understand the following:

- the benefits of reading Scripture each day to transform and renew your mind with spiritual truth
- how to get to know God by reading his Word and discovering what he has to say about himself…and how he sees you!
- how to talk to God and hear from him—to really connect with him through a process we will call "cocooning"
- a bit about Christian meditation and how to journal what God is teaching you in and through this ancient Christian discipline
- the sacraments and how they help you to connect with God
- how prayers of praise unleash the power of God in our lives
- how to share with others what God is doing in your life

Each session of the study includes a description of a stage of the life cycle of the butterfly, an exploration of its spiritual application, an excerpt of a poem by St. John of the Cross, questions for personal reflection or group discussion, suggestions to help you apply what you have just read to your life, a "Renewing Truth" to contemplate during the week, and Scriptures for daily reflection and journaling. At the end of the book you will find additional resources to help you grow spiritually, and to cultivate the habit of "cocooning" with God through prayer and Scripture reading.

For your convenience, on pages 135–137 we have inserted a copy of each week's "Renewing Truth" that can easily be cut out and placed on your mirror, taped to your refrigerator, or tucked into your pocket to help you to remember these scripturally based, life-transforming foundations for living. These little cards are great aids to assist you on your journey to maturity.

WHY JOURNAL?

There are different forms of writing. Some forms are for others to read (public writing), and some are for personal use (private writing). A journal is a form of private writing, a record of our innermost thoughts and feelings, to be shared only with God, a trusted friend, or a spiritual coach. It is a "safe place" to record thoughts and impressions as we read the Scriptures, and to pour out our hearts to God. (Some find it helpful to be able to go back and read earlier impressions as a way to chart their own spiritual growth!)

Journal writing is not meant to impress or enlighten. We simply record the thoughts and impressions that come to us as we read Scripture and learn to listen for God's voice in our hearts. The classical term for this prayerful reading is *lectio divina* ("divine reading"), which is in itself a form of prayer and meditation. Praying through journaling can be a liberating and beautiful means of expression. Your writing can take on the feeling of a love letter or a song and can be accompanied by a heart-wrenching release of emotions.

Do not attempt to censor yourself as you write. Don't worry about spelling or proper grammar. Do not be afraid of writing down how you truly feel—God knows your heart already. Instead, offer yourself—in all your beauty and your brokenness—freely to God and ask him to use your journal to bring you closer to him. Do not be afraid to give it all to God, who can turn our ashes to beauty, heal our deepest wounds, and set us free.

I hope and pray that you will journey with me, each week building a stronger love for God and a deeper desire for him and his ways. You will never regret a step that leads you closer to him.

"Sometimes your only available transportation
is a leap of faith."

—Margaret Shepard

A Miracle of New Creation

The "common" monarch butterfly is anything but common. Of all of God's creatures, the *Danaus plexippus*—especially the North American eastern migrating variety—is among the most baffling to scientists. In fact, its unique migrating habits have even been studied by NASA. Sadly, the monarch is uncommon in another sense as well—it is on the World Wildlife Federation's "near threatened" list of endangered species. As you progress through this study and are inspired mentally and spiritually by this amazing creature, I hope you will want to learn more about how you can help monarchs. Something as simple as planting milkweed in your garden can make a difference.

The monarch has uncanny navigational capabilities as well as a brilliantly designed aeronautic structure. Each of its four wings contains over 1.4 million scales that catch the air as the wings flutter, providing lift and buoyancy. We will learn much more about this captivating creature in the sessions ahead.

For now, let's start at the very beginning. Let's look at the first few moments in the life cycle of the monarch and see what we can draw from this phase of its life to help us along in our own spiritual transformation.

Each year, every North American eastern migrating monarch butterfly follows part of a familiar pattern. Starting in February in their winter home, high in the mountains of central Mexico, adult butterflies start to flutter out of their sleepy, wintery rest to migrate north, find a mate, and then begin a process that will take four generations to complete. By about March, the females lay their eggs—the size of a pinhead! — depositing them one by one on the undersides of milkweed leaves. The adult may die before the eggs hatch, but the eggs are safe on the milkweed leaves, for the plant is poisonous to most predatory insects.

Inside each teeny, tiny egg, God locked everything needed to eventually develop a mature, beautiful butterfly. In a few short days, something fascinating takes place inside this microcosm of life: a baby caterpillar is formed. And within this immature caterpillar body are something called imaginal discs—the microscopic building blocks of the imago, the mature adult butterfly. These undetectable engines of change, master sculptors of sorts, will be just about the only part of the caterpillar that will not later dissolve in the pupa, or chrysalis, stage. They will eventually shape, form, and build the butterfly from the very essence of the caterpillar.

Each of us begins life as a teeny, tiny fertilized egg, safely protected in the womb of our mother. The *Catechism of the Catholic Church* teaches that, through marriage, "spouses share in the creative power and fatherhood of God" (*CCC* 2367). Each person is "created in the image of God" with both a body and a soul (see *CCC* 363).

Life is God's freely given gift to us; each child is an unrepeatable and irreplaceable gift, beloved by God. Each and every fertilized egg is impressed with the very image of God, who created us to know and love him forever.

Does it surprise you to hear that God created you unlike any other creature and wanted you from the first moment you came into existence? No matter what your parents intended—whether they think they "planned" you or you were a beautiful surprise package from God—God always knew when, where, and how you would be born, what you would look like, and all of the circumstances of your birth. And he loved you from the very start.

God says, "You are precious in my sight, and honored, and I love you" (Isaiah 43:4). No matter what your origins or how you came to be, you are precious to God and are meant to be here, now. God has a glorious purpose for your life!

The psalmist writes: "It was you who formed my inward parts; / you knit me together in my mother's womb" (Psalm 139:13). The Church teaches that it is by our baptism that we are filled with God's Holy Spirit. This Spirit is what enables us to grow to maturity to resemble our heavenly Father. His Spirit—unseen and undetected by the human eye—works just as the imaginal discs do inside the immature caterpillar. This Spirit of God is what will eventually produce "an eternal weight of glory" in our lives (2 Corinthians 4:17).

✤ *Thoughts to Ponder*

Take a moment to ponder the following, and journal the thoughts and impressions that arise. If you are taking part in a group study, consider highlighting or marking in the margins points you would like to share with the group.

You were created intentionally. God speaks through his prophet in the Old Testament: "I have called you by name, you are mine" (Isaiah 43:1). No matter how you got here, God made you, knows you, and loves you. Write a bit about who you are and about your first impressions of God. What do you think of God's calling you by name? How do you feel about God's saying that you are his?

....

....

....

....

....

....

....

....

....

....

You were created uniquely. Jesus tells us that "even the hairs of your head are all counted" (Matthew 10:30). Record one thing that makes you unique—something for which you are thankful. (Your uncanny ability to...stand on your head? Be a dog whisperer? Whip up an amazing meal out of a few items in the fridge? Hot-wire a car?)

....

....

....

....

....

....

....

....

....

....

You were created to be loved. Can you think of a time when you felt extremely loved by a parent, grandparent, child, or spouse? Believe it or not, God is longing to show you just that same kind of extreme love! And it is *even greater* than this! Even when we feel supremely unloved and unlovable, God's love never wavers. He is the source of all love. He is Love itself. What do you think about this kind of emotional love coming from God? What does it bring up in your heart?

....

....

....

....

....

....

....

....

....

....

🦋*A Moment with St. John of the Cross*

How gently and lovingly
You awake in my heart,
Where in secret you dwell alone;
And by your sweet breathing,
Filled with good and glory,
How tenderly you swell my heart with love.[1]
—from "The Living Flame of Love"

In this short passage, St. John of the Cross speaks of the "awakening" that takes place within the soul as it first encounters the infinite love of God. What image does this passage bring to mind? How does it remind you of the tiny egg laid bare on the milkweed leaf? Take a moment to journal your thoughts about this. No one needs to see what you write but you and God, who created you not to remain earthbound, but to soar to new heights.

....

....

....

....

....

....

....

....

....

....

✤ *Thoughts for Discussion*

The following questions may be used in a group setting or as additional journaling prompts.

• Scripture tells us: "Do not be conformed to this world, but be transformed by the renewing of your minds" (Romans 12:2). What does this mean?

....

....

....

....

....

....

....

....

....

....

- We are called to renew our minds daily, even moment to moment, by pondering the truth of God's Word. When and how often do you read the Bible? What, if anything, is keeping you from exploring God's Word?

....

....

....

....

....

....

....

....

....

- God wants us to recall that we are his beloved sons and daughters, intentionally and uniquely made. He loves us and intends for us to grow in love and virtue, changing from the inside until we resemble him. In what area of your life do you most need to grow?

....

....

....

....

....

....

....

....

....

....

• God wants the hunger in our hearts to be fully satisfied. What is one thing you could do to get to know God better and to grow in love?

....

....

....

....

....

....

....

....

....

....

• What did the passage from St. John of the Cross say to you about the kind of love God wants from us and the kind of love he has for us?

....

....

....

....

....

....

....

....

....

....

Let's close by asking God to place in each of us a desire to renew our minds to his truth, to get to know him better, and to love him as he truly is…Love itself. Let's be thankful for this incredible gift of life and love and undertake this study with an "attitude of gladitude."

 Prayer

Dear Lord,

Thank you for meeting me right where I am. Thank you for seeking me out, for creating me intentionally and uniquely, and for allowing me to have a relationship with you. Please stir in me the desire to know you more, and give me the grace I need to respond to your divine initiative. I am beginning to understand that my spiritual hunger will be satisfied only if I come to know you and follow your will.

You told us that if we seek you, you will allow yourself to be found: "Ask, and it will be given you; search, and you will find; knock, and the door will be opened for you" (Matthew 7:7). Beginning today, I want to experience your presence in my life. Be with me this week and ignite a spark in me that will grow into a blazing flame of love. Let it consume my deepest fears, darkest sins, and lukewarm apathy. Let me taste the abundant, peaceful, confident, loving, and joyful life that only you can give. Lord, I want only you. Anything less is not worth the asking.

I ask this in the name of the Father, the Son, and the Holy Spirit. Amen.

❧A "Renewing Truth"

Each time I look in the mirror I will say:

"I am intentionally and uniquely made for a relationship with God, who says, 'You are precious in my eyes, and honored, and I love you.'" (Isaiah 43:4)

❧Scriptures for Daily Reflection

You will find a Scripture verse, based on themes from the week's lesson, to ponder each day. Each verse is followed by a short reflection. Take a few minutes to prayerfully read the verse and the reflection, using them as a springboard to launch into a time of prayer with the Lord. Use the journal space to write any thoughts or inspirations that God gives you during these moments of intimacy with him.

"Why should I do this every day," you ask?

Here's why: "My sheep hear my voice. I know them, and they follow me" (John 10:27). Each shepherd has a unique whistle that he uses to call his sheep. If we cannot hear our Shepherd "whistling" in the quiet, we will never hear him in the noise and confusion of this world. As he tells us in Scripture, if we want to know the Master's voice, then we must take the time to listen carefully to find out what his voice sounds like.

Just five minutes of listening and responding each day can change your life. God will feed your soul and transform your spirit through the renewing of your mind to his truth. I pray that you will take a few minutes each day to let the God of love speak to you, and then answer him back. That is what we call prayer.

Day One: Wonderfully Made

I praise you, because I am fearfully and wonderfully made.
Wonderful are your works;
that I know very well. (Psalm 139:14)

Lord, the small, vulnerable butterfly egg is carefully laid on a milkweed leaf because you designed it that way. It is safe there. How wonderful are your works! Help me, Lord, to realize that your same creative genius was at work in me from the moment of my conception, and that you care for me infinitely more because I am made in your image.

Continue the reflection below:

....

....

....

....

....

....

....

....

....

....

❧ *Day Two: In His Image*

So God created humankind in his image,
    in the image of God he created them;
    male and female he created them. (Genesis 1:27)

Butterflies are beautiful. So are sunsets, and crashing waves, and robins'
eggs. You made these things, Lord, and they reflect your glory. But only
men and women are made in your image. Help me to deeply appreciate
this truth about myself and my neighbor.

Continue the reflection below:

....

....

....

....

....

....

....

....

....

....

....

....

❧Day Three: You Know Me

O Lord, you have searched me and known me.
You know when I sit down and when I rise up;
  you discern my thoughts from far away.
You search out my path and my lying down,
  and are acquainted with all my ways.
Even before a word is on my tongue,
  O Lord, you know it completely.
You hem me in, behind and before,
  and lay your hand upon me. (Psalm 139:1–5)

Lord, you are not just "out there" in the universe or "up there" in heaven beyond my reach. No! You are here with me, searching my thoughts, guiding my steps, inspiring my speech, and watching me sleep. Help me to believe that, like St. Paul, "in [you] I live and move and have my being" (Acts 17:28).

Continue the reflection below:

❧*Day Four: Knocking at the Door*

Listen, I am standing at the door, knocking; if you hear my voice
and open the door, I will come in to you and eat with you, and
you with me. (Revelation 3:20)

Lord, the door of my heart is closed when I am preoccupied, worried,
unforgiving, or too busy. But in these moments what I need most is
a sense of your presence. Help me to always hear you knocking, and
give me the grace to open wide the door to my heart, even now as I sit
quietly with you. I open my heart to you. Speak to me Lord.

Continue the reflection below:

✤ Day Five: Child of God

See what love the Father has given us, that we should be called children of God; and that is what we are. (1 John 3:1)

Lord, I am your child, so teach me to depend on you, to count on you to provide for me, and to love you with the simplicity of a child's heart.

Continue the reflection below:

....

....

....

....

....

....

....

....

....

....

✤ Day Six: Redeemed

Do not fear, for I have redeemed you;
I have called you by name, you are mine. (Isaiah 43:1)

Praise to you, Lord, Almighty Redeemer! You have loved me since before my birth. You knew my name before my parents named me. You redeemed me from the cross and called me yours from all eternity. What is there to fear?

Continue the reflection below:

....

....

....

....

....

....

....

....

....

....

❧ *Day Seven: Unforgettable*

Can a woman forget her nursing child,
  or show no compassion for the child of her womb?
Even these may forget,
  yet I will not forget you. (Isaiah 49:15)

Lord, I assume that you, as Master of the Universe, have a lot of things on your mind. But in this verse of Scripture, you promise that you will never forget me. What an awesome truth! I am full of gratitude!

Continue the reflection below:

....

....

....

Feeding the Hunger

Within only four to six short days after the egg is laid, something amazing happens. The minuscule egg on that milkweed leaf hatches, and a tiny creature appears—a caterpillar. As we have all read, caterpillars are very, very hungry!

What the caterpillar eats is of utmost importance. She must eat the right food in order to grow and be healthy. As the monarch caterpillar eats the milkweed plant—the only leaf the that she can eat—her skin is permeated with milkweed juice. Providentially, milkweed is poisonous to most other creatures, including her predators. Since eating the milkweed makes her poisonous as well, the caterpillar can eat to her heart's content and fuel her amazingly rapid growth, all while protected by the milkweed! With each new stage of growth, God gives the caterpillar an upgrade of sorts and takes her closer to her goal of becoming a "new creation." Let's take a closer look.

* * *

The caterpillar grows bigger and stronger so rapidly that she literally outgrows her skin. She must shed her skin several times to accommodate her expanding girth. Her new stages of development are called *instars*. The shedding of a skin is a real mark of maturation in the caterpillar's life.

Once the caterpillar's outer skin has been stretched as much as it can bear by new growth, it splits and she wriggles free. Ahhhh, what relief! The old skin has at last been shed! While the newly exposed layer of skin is still soft and pliable, the caterpillar does the oddest thing: She pumps herself full of air and inflates so that when the new skin hardens, the caterpillar's soft insides will still have room to grow. As the final step of the molting process, the caterpillar eats her newly shed skin. As disgusting as this sounds, the old skin is full of nutrients the caterpillar must digest to make her stronger as she matures.

Have you ever experienced hunger that could not be satisfied with food? Jesus, who came in the flesh and knows what it is to be human, understands that our true hunger is not simply physical. Let's see what God has given us to satisfy our hungry souls

One of the "symptoms" of God's calling us to conversion and a spiritual awakening is a hunger to know all about the things of God. When I felt God calling me into the Church, I listened to podcasts until late into the night, voraciously read books by saints and converts, and spoke to trusted friends about their personal faith experiences. We can equate the "hungry caterpillar" stage with all that we crave on our spiritual journeys.

As Catholics, we receive our first real spiritual food in the Eucharist, or First Holy Communion. Jesus gave us this sacrament to impart his own divine life to us, his Body, Blood, soul, and divinity. (We can also receive spiritual communion if we have not yet been received into the Church or are otherwise unable to receive sacramental communion. We will address this more fully later in the book.) How do we know that this wafer is real food? Because Jesus told us: "I am the bread of life. Whoever comes to me will never be hungry, and whoever believes in me will never be thirsty" (John 6:35). The Eucharist sustains us for life's journey.

Another important source of spiritual nourishment is the Bible, God's Word to us. As we read (or spiritually consume) these sacred words, our hunger is satisfied, as Jesus promised: "One does not live by bread alone, / but by every word that comes forth from the mouth of God" (Matthew 4:4). The Word of God is like milkweed for us. It is nutritious for our souls—true food from heaven that strengthens and protects us.

Just as predators avoid the caterpillar whose skin has become permeated with the milkweed juice that is poisonous to them, so the devil thinks twice about coming too close to us when we are permeated by the graces of the Eucharist, which fill us with God's divine life, and by his Word!

🦋 *Thoughts to Ponder*

Take a moment to ponder the following, and journal the thoughts and impressions that arise. If you are taking part in a group study, consider highlighting or marking in the margins points you would like to share with the group.

We need to be spiritually nourished with the graces of the Eucharist and the truths of God's Word. This spiritual food helps to protect us from the attacks of the enemy—just as the poisonous milkweed protects the monarch caterpillar. However, we must be intent upon feeding properly on the Word of God, trusting in it, and acting upon it in faith, for as Scripture warns us, "Like a roaring lion your adversary the devil prowls around, looking for someone to devour" (1 Peter 5:8). How have you experienced this to be true in your life? Can you recall a time when truths from God's Word protected you from a lie from the enemy?

....

....

....

....

....

....

....

....

....

What "junk food" does the enemy use to distract you from true spiritual nourishment? Our enemy is a liar who does whatever is necessary to distract us from the protective truth of God's Word so that we might fall prey to his schemes. One of his favorite tricks is to entice us to fill up on trashy books or magazines, unsavory entertainment, Internet gossip, or pornography. Has this ever been a problem for you? In what kind of spiritual "junk food" are you most likely to indulge?

....

....

....

....

....

....

....

....

....

....

The good news is that when we feed deeply on the Word of God, it becomes much easier to spot temptation and to avoid it! It also becomes easier to use God's Word as a "sword" in the heat of battle, when we find ourselves being tempted to do what we know is wrong (or not do what we know is right.) We can call to mind fortifying Scripture giving us strength in helping us to fight the good fight. Just as we need to be very careful about what we put into our bodies, we should also be cautious about what we feed our souls. What is one way you could improve the quality of your spiritual "diet"?

....

....

....

....

....

....

....

....

....

....

Once the caterpillar has grown too big for her own skin, she must shed herself. This is what God asks of us when he inspires us to draw closer to him. We "shed ourselves" by letting go of our fears, worries, and resentments—all that is holding us back—and asking the Lord to help us to grow in maturity.

In the book of James, we read: "My brothers, whenever you face trials of any kind, consider it nothing but joy, because you know that the testing of your faith produces endurance; and let endurance have its full effect, so that you may be mature and complete, lacking in nothing" (James 1:2–4).

Fear and an unwillingness to forgive are two things that can really stunt our spiritual growth. God will work mightily to root these out of our souls if we humbly turn everything over to him. He can do things in us that we cannot even imagine, like helping us to forgive the unforgivable and setting us free from past hurts that once paralyzed us. Sometimes this "shedding" can be painful, but it is all for our good. All he asks of us is to be willing to let him do the work inside of us. What are some fears and wounds that you sense God is asking you to "shed"?

....

....

....

....

....

....

....

....

....

....

Just as the caterpillar "inflates" herself in order to stretch her new skin and give herself room to grow, God pumps us full of his Holy Spirit to "inflate" us when we turn to him in prayer. Filled with the Holy Spirit, we have the capacity to handle any circumstance.

Listen to the words of St. Paul: "I can do *all things* [emphasis mine] through him who strengthens me" (Philippians 4:13). What was true for St. Paul is true for us as well. We must have faith during these often challenging and potentially uncomfortable growth spurts. By doing our part—consuming what is spiritually good for us (the Eucharist and the Word of God), avoiding what is bad for us (spiritual junk food), and participating in the process (seeking out the sacrament of reconciliation, forgiving others, and self-acceptance)—we open ourselves to true growth caused by the miraculous grace of God.

What is one area of your life in which you think God is asking you to grow right now? Write a short note to God in the space below, entrusting this area of your life into his care.

....

....

....

....

....

....

....

....

....

....

Just as the caterpillar eats her own shed skin, we too must learn to shed our sinfulness, swallow our pride, forgive others, and accept ourselves. Maturity can be painful, requiring us to leave behind what we've outgrown, rid ourselves of bad habits, or even eat our own words in a gesture of repentance or humility. By dying on the cross for us, Jesus provided everything we need to be set free from these old, sinful habits. He lives to forgive and restore us through the sacrament of reconciliation (see appendix two.) In that sacrament, we can bring to him the worst of ourselves and allow him to redeem it all for his glory. He forgives us and strengthens our resolve to stop sinning.

Most Catholics understand the aspect of forgiveness in the sacrament of reconciliation, but many underestimate how much spiritual fortification it gives us. Here's what the *Catechism* says:

> The whole power of the sacrament of Penance consists in restoring us to God's grace and joining us with him in an intimate friendship. (*CCC* 1468)

When we receive this sacrament with a contrite and open heart, we receive a tremendous gift: We are reconciled to God, restored into intimate friendship with him in a way that brings about "peace and serenity of conscience with strong spiritual consolation" (*CCC* 1468).

Indeed, the sacrament of reconciliation with God brings about a true "spiritual resurrection," a restoration of the dignity and blessings of the life of the children of God, of which the most precious is friendship with God.

Have you experienced this sense of peace and release from confession? Is there any part of your life right now that needs the healing and strengthening graces of this sacrament? Incredible as it may seem, because of his great love for us, God is able to take the worst parts of our past and use them for our good, for our growth, and for his own glory—if we let him. As St. Paul tells us: "We know that all things work together for good for those who love God, who are called according to his purpose" (Romans 8:28).

Is there a part of your past that you find hard to let go of, or that you find it difficult to believe God would want to forgive? Read Romans 8:28 again slowly. Write it in the space below, underlining or decorating the words that are most meaningful to you:

This week you may want to try connecting with God through the sacrament of reconciliation and by receiving him in the Eucharist. Reconciliation is a "spiritual spa treatment" for Catholics. It exfoliates sin from the soul and slathers on grace. Try going to a daily Mass this week. Even if you cannot receive sacramental communion, you can still receive communion spiritually by sitting in the presence of the Lord and asking him for the graces he wants to give you through prayer. Consider making an appointment with a priest to discuss your situation. If you are hungry, Jesus wants to satisfy that hunger.

In the meantime, remember that spiritual communion prepares us to receive sacramental communion by keeping our hearts turned toward Christ. Below is a prayer for spiritual communion that anyone can offer, at any time, connecting your heart and soul through prayer to our loving Lord. This "Act of Oblation" was written by St. Faustina Kowalska, to whom Jesus entrusted the revelation of his Divine Mercy.

❧ Prayer for Spiritual Communion

Jesus-Host, whom I have this very moment received into my heart, in this union with you I offer myself to the Heavenly Father as a sacrificial host, abandoning myself totally and completely to the most merciful holy will of my God. From today onward, your will, Lord, is my food. You have my whole being; dispose of me as you please.... I no longer fear any of your inspirations, nor do I probe anxiously to see where they will lead me.... I have placed all my trust in your will which is, for me, love and mercy itself.[2]

28

❧ *A Moment with St. John of the Cross*

O lamps of fire!
In whose splendors
The deep caverns of feeling,
Once obscured and blind,
Now give forth, so rarely, so exquisitely,
Both warmth and light to their beloved. [3]
—from "The Living Flame of Love"

In this passage, St. John of the Cross speaks of the Flame of Love that warms and guides us as we gather strength to emerge from the darkness. What comes to mind when you read of "lamps of fire" in the "deep caverns of feeling"? Consider the caterpillar repeatedly bursting her tight old skin, then "puffing up" inside her new skin. Where do you feel a sense of urgency to push your limits in order to grow? Take a few moments to journal your thoughts. Invite God to enlighten your mind and soul, "once obscured and blind."

....

....

....

....

....

....

....

....

❧ *Thoughts for Discussion*

The following questions may be used in a group setting or as additional journaling prompts.

Spiritually speaking, we truly do become what we eat! As we consume the Eucharist (or receive Christ in spiritual communion through prayer) and ponder God's Word, the Bible, we grow spiritually and are transformed by God's grace. God has chosen us to become *holy*—not out of grudging duty, but in response to his love for us.

In the first chapter of Ephesians, St. Paul writes: "Blessed be the God and Father of our Lord Jesus Christ, who has blessed us in Christ with every spiritual blessing in the heavenly places, just as he chose us in Christ before the foundation of the world *to be holy and blameless before him in love* [emphasis mine]" (Ephesians 1:3–4).

• What does *holiness* mean to you? In his book *Interior Freedom,* Father Jacques Philippe defines holiness as "the possibility of growing indefinitely in love for God and our brothers and sisters."[4] How do you respond to, or how would you build upon, this definition?

• Do you think "holiness" is attractive? Can you give an example of someone you know whose actions inspire you to be a better person— someone who inspires you to be holy?

....

....

....

....

....

....

....

• We have a God-given appetite that makes us hungry for love and attracted to goodness. Sometimes we resort to spiritual "junk food" in order to fill that hunger—but somehow it always leaves us unsatisfied. What spiritual junk food do you have a hard time resisting? Discuss the consequences of bingeing on these things. What are some criteria for choosing how to satisfy our God-given longing for love?

....

....

....

....

....

....

....

• God wants to free us and expand our capacity to grow in friendship with him through the sacrament of reconciliation. What is your experience with the sacrament? Do you go regularly? Why or why not?

....

....

....

....

....

....

....

• Read aloud the passage from St. John of the Cross. What is the "warmth and light" God wants to give to us in order to help us spiritually mature?

....

....

....

....

....

....

....

Let's close by asking God to give us courage to see ourselves as he sees us and to let go of anything that is holding us back from becoming the women he created us to be. We don't need to be afraid because we are surrounded by Love himself.

Prayer

Dear Lord,

Thank you for meeting me right where I am. Thank you for the gift of the Eucharist—*you*, here for me in the sacrament. Help me to come to a greater understanding of this mystery as I continue to seek you. Thank you for your divine Word, which nourishes my soul, gives wisdom to my heart and mind, and teaches me about you and how I am to live.

Finally, thank you for the sacrament of reconciliation that makes "all things new" (Revelation 21:5). Please take my past and use even my worst mistakes for your glory. Give me all I need to become all you dream for me to be.

I ask this in the name of the Father, the Son, and the Holy Spirit. Amen.

A "Renewing Truth"

Each time I eat food, I will remind myself:

> I am what I eat. Fill me with you, Lord, even as "the disciples were filled with joy and with the Holy Spirit" (Acts 13:52).

Scriptures for Daily Reflection

As in the last session, you will find in this section a Scripture verse, based on themes for this week's lesson, to ponder each day. Take a few minutes to prayerfully read the verse and the reflection, using them as a springboard to launch into a time of personal prayer. Use the journal space to write any thoughts or inspirations that God gives to you during these moments of quiet intimacy with him.

✤ Day One: Bread of Life

> I am the bread of life. Whoever comes to me will never be hungry,
> and whoever believes in me will never be thirsty. (John 6:35)

Lord, in this verse of Scripture you call yourself the bread of life. You want to nourish me. You promise to sustain me, so that I will never hunger or thirst. Give me a real spiritual hunger. I open myself to your grace to drink in your goodness.

Continue the reflection below:

....

....

....

....

....

....

....

....

....

....

✤ Day Two: Taste and See

> Taste and see that the LORD is good… (Psalm 34:9, NABRE)

Your words, Lord, are "sweeter than honey to my mouth!" (Psalm 119:103). Your words bring me sweet peace, joy, and true happiness.

What good words will you speak to me today in these moments of prayer?

Continue the reflection below:

....

....

....

....

....

....

....

....

....

Day Three: Forgive and Forget

As far as the east is from the west, / so far he removes our transgressions from us. (Psalm 103:12)

Lord, this truth is a great consolation to me. I can bring my worst self to you, and in your infinite mercy, you forgive and forget my sin. You even have the power to bring good out of my mistakes, for your glory. Praise to you, Lord of mercy and peace, for bringing blessing even out of these situations in my life!

Continue the reflection below:

....

....

....

....

....

....

....

....

....

....

❧ Day Four: Testing Faith

No testing has overtaken you that is not common to everyone.
God is faithful, and he will not let you be tested beyond your
strength; but with the testing he will also provide a way out so
that you may be able to endure it. (1 Corinthians 10:13)

Lord, you promise to strengthen me to face my difficulties. I know that
you are faithful and that you bless any suffering, large or small, that
I offer back to you. Your cross suffuses my sufferings with profound
meaning, turning my pain into a source of spiritual healing for myself
and others. Help me to bear these areas of pain in my life, patiently and
without complaining. Thank you, Lord.

Continue the reflection below:

....

....

....

....

....

....

....

....

....

....

❧*Day Five: Filled with the Spirit*

Be careful then how you live, not as unwise people but as wise, making the most of the time, because the days are evil. So do not be foolish, but understand what the will of the Lord is. Do not get drunk on wine, for that is debauchery; but be filled with the Spirit. (Ephesians 5:15–18)

Lord, I want to feast on you in the Eucharist and the Word, but I am surrounded by some pretty tasty temptations that distract me and attract me! Help me to develop my spiritual taste buds until you alone fulfill all of my desires. Please take away my desire for these lesser things…

Continue the reflection below:

....

....

....

....

....

....

....

....

....

....

❧Day Six: Think about These Things

Finally, beloved, whatever is true, whatever is honorable, whatever is just, whatever is pure, whatever is pleasing, whatever is commendable, if there is any excellence and if there is anything worthy of praise, think about these things. Keep on doing the things that you have learned and received and heard and seen in me, and the God of peace will be with you. (Philippians 4:8–9)

Lord, open my eyes to the truth, the beauty, and the virtue that you will place in my life this day. I don't want to miss a thing! Here are some of the things I have noticed already today…

Continue the reflection below:

....

....

....

....

....

....

....

....

❧ *Day Seven: Confess Our Sins*

If we confess our sins, he who is faithful and just and will forgive us our sins and cleanse us from all unrighteousness. (1 John 1:9)

Do you ever become discouraged by how little progress you seem to make in conquering certain stubborn sins or by certain chapters of your past that leave you feeling condemned and hopeless? Take to heart the words of Fr. Jacques Philippe, who says we should make an act of faith and hope such as this one: "Thank you, my God, for ALL my past. I firmly believe you can draw good out of everything I have lived through. I want to have no regrets, and I resolve today to begin from zero, with exactly the same trust as though my past history were made up of nothing but faithfulness and holiness."[5] This act of faith pleases God and can liberate you from the accusations of the evil one, leaving you free to focus on the more immediate concerns keeping you from growing in grace. About these and any other sins, you can offer the following prayer:

> You have revealed yourself, Lord, as a God of mercy. That means I need not fear punishment or retribution for those sins I leave wholly with you in confession. Emboldened by my reliance on your merciful heart, I ask you to help me remember my wrongdoings today, so that I might make a good confession and receive peace and pardon. I ask this in the name of the Father, the Son, and the Holy Spirit. Amen.

Continue the reflection below:

....

....

....

Transforming in a Quiet Place

When we left the hungry caterpillar, she was munching her way through lots of milkweed and outgrowing her skin every couple of days. She is now about two weeks old and has reached two inches in length—about two thousand times her original size. She's ready for the next stage of development.

This next stage of metamorphosis is absolutely baffling to scientists. There are different theories about how and why it takes place, but no one knows for sure. Such a mystery!

* * *

The full-grown caterpillar stops eating milkweed and leaves the plant—the only home she's known—to find a new, safe place to pupate. She secures herself with a "silk button" woven from a gland right below her mouth and, with her claspers holding tight, begins to hang upside down. Next, she releases the claspers so that she is suspended upside down, hanging by a silk thread in a "J" shape for as long as a day. Imagine her view of the heavens from this perspective!

Her fifth and final instar (stage between skin sheddings) has revealed a strange new type of skin and a shape perfectly suited to what comes next: the pupal (chrysalis) stage. The chrysalis forms a hard, protective coating or shell around the soft, vulnerable creature, enclosing the pupa into her own little world to allow her to transform into the mature butterfly that she was always meant to be.

[Note: Technically, as stated, a monarch is transformed within the confines of a hardened protein shell called a chrysalis, and a moth within a soft spun silk cocoon. I've taken a bit of poetic license and used the terms interchangeably—after all, "cocooning" is a much softer image and easier to say than "chrysalising"!]

Once inside the chrysalis, the caterpillar does not simply sprout wings. She begins to break down into a "protein soup" that will be used to form the butterfly. Those microscopic imaginal discs (see session one) are just about the only part of the former caterpillar that will not dissolve. Particular imaginal discs will begin to vibrate at a frequency that excites the other discs, until they are all pulsating at the same frequency and begin to merge together to create all of the required and unique body parts of the new creature. The caterpillar literally disintegrates in order to be recreated into the butterfly.

Amazingly, the butterfly will be made from the same physical material and have the exact same DNA as the caterpillar, but she will now be a complete and beautifully mature version of herself. Any injuries or imperfections she had as a caterpillar (a missing leg or antenna, for example), are made new during this meta-morphic process. All she must do is to be patient and wait for all of her parts to be adequately formed.

We can learn quite a bit about what God has in mind for our meta-morphosis by considering the caterpillar entering the pupa stage. Caterpillars are transformed within the confines of their chrysalises. We remember from the introduction that each of us is to be trans-formed "*by the renewing of your minds,* so that you may discern what is the will of God—what is good and acceptable and perfect" (Romans 12:2, emphasis mine). If we want to truly be like God, to be changed to resemble him, we must be renewed from the inside out by learning his truths.

In order for this renewal to happen, we must first be willing to step away from this world, find a safe place, settle in, hang on, and then let go. Like the caterpillar, we must try to see life from a heavenly perspec-tive. We don't have to hang upside down, but establishing a regular place of prayer can be helpful. I like going to the Adoration chapel, or sitting inside the church, or being outside in the midst of nature, or tucking myself away in a comfy chair at home. We need to have a regular time and place where we can sit undisturbed and be with God…alone with him.

In our place of prayer, we welcome the silence and enclose ourselves in it. We bring all that we are, offering it to be used in the process of transformation—the good, the not so good, and—let's be honest—the ugly. St. Teresa of Avila speaks of "the great favor" we are given when we are able to see "how all things are seen in God, and how within Himself He contains them all….since it is within God Himself…we dwell…"—even our own sinfulness.[6]

When we give ourselves to God, and ask his Holy Spirit to come and work in us to change and mold us from the inside out, we can begin to become a new creation. We bring our good works, our gifts and abilities, our weaknesses and strengths, even our pride and selfishness to him, inviting him to take what needs to be "dissolved" so that something more beautiful can appear. God is so loving and creative. He never wastes a thing. Only he can make good out of bad and turn meager loaves and fishes (see Mark 6:41–42) into great abundance. He is in the business of redemption and blessing.

Just as the caterpillar must find a safe place to hang while she undergoes her big change, so must we hang on to God, our safe place. We can confidently attach ourselves to him, knowing that he will never let us go or stop loving us; and because of this truth, we are able to stop clinging to this world and detach. We can "float," tethered to our safe Anchor. During our cocooning time with him, God will cause a lovely protective coating of absolute peace to form around us as he works deep inside of us. He is a safe and sure stronghold, so we trust in him.

And just as the caterpillar's imaginal discs start pulsating within her during her metamorphosis, the gifts of his Holy Spirit that God gave us at baptism begin to quicken within us when we cocoon with God.

When we read or hear truth, it excites our soul, and the new creature we were always meant to be takes shape. "Deep calls to deep" is how the psalmist puts it (Psalm 42:7). Our souls begin to stir, and our hearts begin to burn. "You will know the truth," Jesus said, "and the truth will make you free!" (John 8:32).

So, as we sit daily cocooning with God, reading his Word and journaling about what we feel he is saying to us (which is in itself a form of prayer), we…

- offer ourselves to him to be transformed by his truth
- ask him to take care of our needs and the concerns of those we love
- sit quietly in his presence, soaking up his light and love

Real change is taking place as we cocoon with God, whether we feel it or not. We can't help it! The more time we spend gazing at him, and he at us, the more we are transformed.

One caveat: Transformation takes time. It doesn't happen in the same way for any two people. And believe it or not, we may undergo many, many metamorphoses before we become a completed new creature. It is almost as if the Lord is working on one little body part at a time. But we can have faith that, little by little, a beautiful butterfly will emerge!

But the key to our transformation is the same for each of us: God does the work of transforming us to the degree that we are willing to dissolve ourselves, our ways, our schedules, our desires, and so forth, and be open to the new and beautiful, sweet and gentle way of God. If we "let go" and trust God to do what he needs to do in us, he changes our hearts so that the process of transformation becomes, not drudgery to do as he asks, but a delight in order to please him.

Remember, the butterfly has the exact same DNA as the caterpillar. That means that the caterpillar had a butterfly heart deep within her from the very beginning—she just didn't know it! The Lord sees our butterfly heart, the one we will grow into as we spiritually mature. When we present ourselves to the Lord, he gently and beautifully does all that's necessary: He works with what we give him. If there is brokenness, he fixes it. He makes us a more fabulous version of ourselves! It is all his doing. And it is very, very good.

✤ Thoughts to Ponder

Take a moment to ponder the following, and journal the thoughts and impressions that arise. If you are taking part in a group study, consider highlighting or marking in the margins points you would like to share with the group.

Each of us needs a "cocoon" of space and quiet in order to grow. Just as the caterpillar must remove herself from the only home she has ever known (her milkweed leaf) and anchor herself upside down in a quiet place in order to advance to the pupa stage, so we are called to remove ourselves from the familiar hustle and bustle of life and set aside some time and space to seek a new and heavenly perspective on life. God invites us each day to an intimate time of conversation with him!

How often do you set aside quiet time to talk with the Lord? Where is your favorite place for prayer? What essentials do you think you need in order to foster a daily habit of prayer—what do you need to do to create your own "cocoon" with God?

....

....

....

....

....

Through prayer, the Lord works with our spiritual DNA to bring forth a new creation! He does not change the essence of who we are, because we are precious in his eyes. Instead, he welcomes, heals, renews, and restores us so that we reach our full potential.

As the renewal begins, God begins to open our eyes and speak to our hearts so that the "fleshly" part of us loosens its grip, and we grow more willing to leave behind bad habits, vices, and sin. St. Paul explains why this is necessary in his letter to the Romans: "For those who live according to the flesh set their minds on the things of the flesh, but those who live according to the Spirit set their minds on the things of the Spirit. To set the mind on the flesh is death, but to set the mind on the Spirit is life and peace" (Romans 8:5–6).

This "letting go" can be painful at first. But the Lord, gentle as he is, encourages us with spiritual encouragements. He always gives us more in return than we could ever give him! Reflect quietly for a few minutes, and make a note of the blessings—large and small—that you have experienced this week. Write down any little miracles—(miraclettes!) "touches of the divine"—that you find particularly wonderful or encouraging.

....

....

....

....

....

....

....

....

....

....

✤ *A Moment with St. John of the Cross*

O Living flame of fire!

That tenderly wounds my soul

In its deepest center! Since

Now you are not oppressive,

Now Consummate! if it be your will:

Tear through the veil of this sweet encounter![7]

—from "The Living Flame of Love"

In this passage, St. John of the Cross speaks of the "wounding" of love, when God so tenderly and deeply touches our hearts that it makes us long for greater union with him. What does this passage say will happen as we draw away to spend time with God? Is there anything you sense God is asking you to let go of, so that you are better able to receive his grace in order to be transformed?

....

....

....

....

....

....

....

....

🦋 *Thoughts for Discussion*

The following questions may be used in a group setting or as additional journaling prompts.

Committing to daily prayer takes personal sacrifice—and promises rich rewards! What does Scripture say we can expect from time we spend with the Lord in prayer? Read these verses aloud, and reflect on each of them:

• "If you remain in my word, you will truly be my disciples, and you will know the truth and, the truth will set you free" (John 8:31–32). What is the connection between knowing God's Word and spiritual growth and freedom?

....

....

....

....

....

....

• "But strive first for the kingdom of God and his righteousness, and all these things will be given to you as well" (Matthew 6:33). What is the connection between growing to be more like Jesus (growing in holiness) and experiencing lasting happiness?

....

....

....

....

....

....

• "Because he clings to me I will deliver him; because he knows my name I will set him on high. He will call upon me and I will answer; I will be with him in distress; I will deliver him and give him honor. With length of days I will satisfy him, and fill him with my saving power." (Psalm 91:14–16) What is the connection between clinging to God in prayer and being delivered in our distress with his saving power?

....

....

....

....

....

....

For our closing prayer today, we are going to introduce a spiritual exercise called "palms down, palms up," to help us quiet our minds and focus on the Lord. This prayer practice, like all authentic prayer practices, has a single purpose: to draw us closer to the heart of Christ.

 ## *Prayer*

Make the Sign of the Cross and say, "In the name of the Father, the Son, and the Holy Spirit." Once you've read through the directions, close your eyes and silently place your hands in your lap. Ask God to fill your heart and to meet with you in that moment.

Turn your palms downward, fingers curled gently under. You are in the position of giving. Silently open your hands and give to God your "laundry list" of all that is on your heart and mind: cares, concerns, and praises. These can be prayers for yourself or your family or friends. Name them all (one to two minutes).

Now place your palms upward. You are in the position of receiving. Ask God to fill you with his light, peace, and joy—all of *himself*. You need not say or think of anything. Just sit and soak him in. Picture yourself in the presence of our heavenly Father, being filled to your deepest core with his light and love, connecting to him (one to two minutes or more).

If you are easily distracted, ask the Holy Spirit to help you refocus your mind on the present moment of being with God. When you are ready, thank God for all that he has done for you, and for filling you with his Holy Spirit.

Close with the Sign of the Cross.

✤A "Renewing Truth"

Every time I put on my clothes or coat, I will remind myself that you wrap me in your love, you are safe, and you are transforming me by your love every minute of each new day. I will say:

"He must increase, but I must decrease." (John 3:30)

✤Scriptures for Daily Reflection

Below are Scripture passages, based on themes from this week's lesson, to read each day. Each verse is followed by a short reflection. Take a few minutes to prayerfully read the verse and the reflection, using them as a springboard to launch into a time of prayer with the Lord. Use the journal space to write any thoughts or inspirations that God gives you during these moments of intimacy with him.

This week, after you pray with Scripture, you may want to take two or three minutes to practice the "palms down, palms up" prayer.

✤Day One: In the Morning

O Lord, in the morning you hear my voice;
in the morning I plead my case to you, and watch.

For you are not a God who delights in wickedness;
evil will not sojourn with you. (Psalm 5:3–4)

Lord, I can't imagine being faithful to a set time of prayer every morning. I feel sure that life will get in the way. But I'm going to try because this Scripture says that you will hear my voice. Here is what I want to say to you today…

Continue the reflection below:

....

....

....

....

....

....

....

....

....

....

❧*Day Two: Gaining Christ*

Yet whatever gains I had, these I have come to regard as loss because of Christ. More than that, I regard everything as loss because of the surpassing value of knowing Christ Jesus my Lord. For his sake I have suffered the loss of all things, and I regard them as rubbish, in order that I may gain Christ.... (Philippians 3:7–8)

St. Paul testifies to us that knowing you is of "surpassing value." I want to experience that, Lord. I want to get so close to you that knowing you is worth "the loss of all things." I praise you, Lord. I want you to become everything to me!

Continue the reflection below:

....

....

....

....

....

....

....

....

....

....

Day Three: Withdraw and Pray

But [Jesus] would withdraw to deserted places and pray. (Luke 5:16)

As a Christian, I'm called to imitate you, Lord. You withdrew from the crowds to pray, even though their needs were great and you loved them dearly. I want to find the time to pray regularly, and I want to be faithful to this commitment. Help me to see that this is the most important work I can do each day for the good of those I love. Thank you for the grace to persevere even though so many things are weighing on my mind…

Continue the reflection below:

....

....

....

....

....

....

....

....

❧*Day Four: I Behold Your Face*

As for me, I shall behold your face in righteousness;
   when I awake I shall be satisfied, beholding your likeness.
   (Psalm 17:15)

Lord, your gaze is always upon me, even as I sleep. You anticipate even more than I do that day when I will see you face-to-face. You are an awesome God! Please give me the grace to empty my mind and heart of distractions. Let me behold your face.

Continue the reflection below:

....

....

....

....

....

....

....

....

....

....

❧Day Five: My Soul Thirsts

O God, you are my God, I seek you,
  my soul thirsts for you;
my flesh faints for you,
  as in a dry and weary land where there is no water.
So I have looked upon you in the sanctuary,
  beholding your power and glory (Psalm 63:1–2)

I wish I could say that my flesh faints and my soul thirsts for you. That doesn't always feel like the truth. Sometimes I doubt. Sometimes I am sad. Sometimes I am baffled by life's circumstances. Bless me, Lord, and increase my desire for you. Your power and glory are everywhere, if I can lift my eyes from my own troubles and seek you out.

Continue the reflection below:

....

....

....

....

....

....

....

....

....

....

❧ *Day Six: Great Is Your Faithfulness*

The steadfast love of the LORD never ceases,

  his mercies never come to an end;

they are new every morning;

  great is your faithfulness. (Lamentations 3:22–23)

Lord, this Scripture reminds me that you await my presence each morning. You long for these quiet moments more than I do. I want to learn something "new every morning." Help me to be faithful as you are faithful. What do you want to teach me this morning, Lord?

  Continue the reflection below:

....

....

....

....

....

....

....

....

....

....

✤Day Seven: Seek Me Diligently

I love those who love me,

and those who seek me diligently find me. (Proverbs 8:17)

What a short but powerful verse of Scripture! You promise I will find you when I seek you in prayer. Be real to me, Lord. Today, in this moment, please give me a reassuring experience of your love. Please be near to me, here and now.

Continue the reflection below:

....

....

....

....

....

....

....

....

....

....

....

Practicing the Virtues

Hanging out upside down in a protective cocoon, relishing peace and quiet—what's not to like? But this silent paradise, like so many others, is not destined to last for our little pupa. One early morning, which the butterfly knows instinctively is the best time to emerge, the once seemingly lifeless chrysalis begins to wiggle. Soon, after a great struggle, a sparkling jewel begins to emerge (eclose) from her tiny treasure chest.

However, she is not quite ready to take on the world. In order to break free, the butterfly must use her newly generated parts and push with all of her might to be released from her shell. If the butterfly does not engage in this difficult but necessary struggle, she will never have the strength to fly.

* * *

Once she breaks free of the chrysalis, the moist and helpless butterfly, having a very full abdomen and crumpled wings, emerges to complete the development process. She climbs to a vertical position and pumps life-giving fluid down into her wings so that they will be fully extended and "sky-worthy." While this is happening, the butterfly's proboscis (coiled tongue), which formed in two parts during metamorphosis, will be zipped together as she coils and uncoils it until it is fused to form a drinking straw with which she will sip flower nectar.

When her wings are fully extended and dry, the butterfly has reached the imago stage—full maturity. But she must continue to exercise her wings, again and again, until she is strong enough for takeoff.

As was emphasized in session three, if we are going to take on the world, the best way to prepare is to connect to our power source: God. If we make prayer our first priority first thing in the morning, we will be ready for whatever life throws at us as we continue our journey toward spiritual maturity (total transformation). Getting "up and at 'em" is not easy—just as it requires a struggle for the butterfly to emerge from the chrysalis, we must often fight the urge to remain in the safety and warmth of our comfortable beds or resist answering texts and emails or other distractions that might keep us from meeting with God. But what glory awaits us once we've made the commitment to regular morning prayer!

The butterfly must go vertical, pointing upward during this stage of her transformation. While at this point she is not at all what she used to be, she is still not quite what she will be. We too must point heavenward. What does that mean? It means that we must be forming our hearts and minds intentionally to know, love, and serve God. In other words, we must grow in *virtue*. But what is that? The *Catechism* teaches us that "a virtue is an habitual and firm disposition to do the good. It allows the person not only to perform good acts, but to give the best of himself" (*CCC* 1803).

In order to truly grow to resemble our heavenly Father, the practice of both *human* and *theological* virtues is required (which we explore further in appendix three). Human virtues form the soul with the habits that mold our moral behavior and help us to control our passions and avoid sin. Virtues guide our conduct, helping us to make wise choices, leading us toward freedom based on self-control and the joy that comes in living a good moral life. Compassion, responsibility, self-discipline, honesty, loyalty, friendship, courage, and perseverance are examples of desirable virtues for sustaining a happy and good moral life.

All human virtues are clustered around four primary *cardinal* virtues; the term comes from the Latin word *cardo,* meaning "hinge." The cardinal virtues are:

- *prudence*, which helps us to choose wisely
- *justice*, which helps us to choose selflessly
- *fortitude*, which helps us to choose courageously and
- *temperance*, which helps us to choose responsibly, according to what we need rather than what we want

While we first learn to appreciate these virtues by witnessing the good example of others, we cultivate virtuous habits, not by observing them, but through practice. The frequent repetition of virtuous acts establishes a pattern of virtuous behavior, and the more we practice virtue, the stronger the instinct grows within us to act in morally good ways.

Just as the monarch must exercise her wings so that in time she will be strong enough to fly, we must practice virtue in order to become spiritually strong.

❧ *Thoughts to Ponder*

Take a moment to ponder the following, and journal the thoughts and impressions that arise. If you are taking part in a group study, consider highlighting or marking in the margins points you would like to share with the group.

Spiritual growth or transformation takes grace, time, and practice. Thankfully, God does not ask us to do anything that he does not give us grace and strength to do. His Holy Spirit makes our spiritual growth possible the way the life-giving fluid that courses through the wings of the butterfly makes flight possible. And just as the butterfly must move her wings so that they become fluid filled, we must "exercise" virtue so that our souls are fully fortified by the grace that flows to us from the Holy Spirit.

The *Catechism* has this to say about the purpose of virtue:

The virtuous person tends toward the good with all his sensory and spiritual powers; he pursues the good and chooses it in concrete actions.

The goal of a virtuous life is to become like God. (*CCC* 1803)

This last line especially reminds us why pursuing virtue is so important. Just as the butterfly continues her formation outside of the chrysalis, so we are formed out in the world. God uses our everyday life experiences to help us grow in virtue. What may seem to be annoyances or even temptations can, in his hands, strengthen us in virtue as we practice patience, cheerfulness, fortitude, or self-discipline. What recent experiences have you had in which you've been given the opportunity to practice human virtues?

....

....

....

....

....

....

....

....

....

....

Even the name of the adult stage of the butterfly, imago, *points to our own purpose and calling. Imago* is the name of the adult stage of a butterfly; *imago Dei* is Latin for "image of God." *Imago* signifies maturity, or what God "imagined" you to be when he created you. Scripture reminds us that we are ultimately created in the imago/image of God:

So God created humankind in his image,

in the image of God he created them;

male and female he created them. (Genesis 1:27)

Our Father wants us to become the best version of ourselves. All of our practice of virtue, strengthened by the Holy Spirit, has as its end our total transformation. We are made in the imago/image of God, and he intends for us to grow up to be just like him, imaging his love in the world as his beloved children.

How do you bear the "image of God" in your world?

....

....

....

....

....

....

....

....

....

....

God wants something else as well: he wants to be united with us not only in heaven, but starting right now! For human beings, made in the image of God, to be fully mature is to be in union with God. He longs for this union, and in the deepest core of our primal being, we long for it too. This union is the purpose for which we were created, our surest source of happiness and joy.

Progressing in our union with Christ takes time, of course. But each time we pray, each time we choose God's will over our own, each time we die to self, we become more united with Christ. This is the way that leads to the perfect union we will experience in heaven!

As noted, when the butterfly first hatches, her wings are not quite strong and full enough to soar. She must be patient even though she is elated to be a new creation! Likewise, God is at work in us, blessing our efforts to live virtuously. And every time we cooperate with his grace—each and every time we say, "Yet, not my will but yours be done" (Luke

22:42)—our wings are being strengthened so that we will be able to soar with God!

Do you want to be fully united to God? What does that mean to you right now? Where do you see God at work in your life, drawing you to full maturity and ever closer to him?

....

....

....

....

....

....

....

....

....

....

A Moment with St. John of the Cross

The tranquil night
At the time of the rising dawn,
Silent music,
Sounding solitude,
The supper that refreshes, and deepens love.[8]
—from "The Spiritual Canticle"

In this poem, the Bridegroom speaks to his Beloved, calling her close to himself. As each morning breaks, the restful solitude of "tranquil night" gives way to the light and activity. Just as the monarch has been in its time of quiet transformation, with the rising dawn comes the silent symphony of a flutter of newly formed wings. What does this passage say to you about the spiritual life and the connection between spending time in tranquil, loving rest, with God and being refreshed in order to prepare to soar?

....

....

....

....

....

....

....

....

....

❧ Thoughts for Discussion

The following questions may be used in a group setting or as additional journaling prompts. You can find answers to the first question below as well as other information about the virtues in appendix three.

For most of us, the language of virtue is not a part of our daily vocabulary. Words like *prudence, justice, fortitude,* and *temperance* (the four cardinal virtues) don't roll off the tongue, and we may even wonder why we would want to put them into practice!

• Do you *desire* virtue? Do you want to live well and teach your children to be good? If so, an understanding of virtue is absolutely essential. Take a look at this brief list of virtues. See how many you can define or describe—and how many more you can add to the list! Then turn to appendix three to check your work (or you can read more about the human virtues in the *Catechism*, 1803–1811).

Prudence

Justice

Fortitude

Temperance

Mercy

Forgiveness

....

....

....

....

....

....

• What are some modern interpretations for these virtues, and where are they evident (either by their presence or by their absence) in our culture?

....

....

....

....

....

....

....

• What virtues are exercised by the habit of regular morning prayer?

....

....

....

....

....

• What are some of the "side effects" of practicing virtue? (For example, if we are practicing one virtue, does it become easier or more difficult to grow in virtue in other areas—and why? How does your practicing virtue help others to grow spiritually?) Write down an instance when another's good example influenced your behavior or the actions of those around you.

....

....

....

....

....

In closing, let's invite the Holy Spirit to continue working in us, to help us grow strong in virtue—and to draw to our attention examples of courageous virtue to admire and emulate!

Prayer

Dear Lord,

Thank you for meeting me right where I am. Thank you for the gift of struggles, which you use to help me grow stronger in virtue as the Holy Spirit fills me and "pumps up my wings." Please give me the desire to be virtuous and the strength to live virtuously. Thank you for the virtuous people you send my way to walk alongside me and encourage me. Even when things don't go my way or my timing is different from yours, please help me always to say, "Jesus, I trust in you."

I ask this in the name of the Father, the Son, and the Holy Spirit. Amen.

A "Renewing Truth"

Every time I must wait in line, on hold, in traffic, or for the microwave to ding, and when someone is standing on my last nerve, I will say, "I am growing in virtue. Jesus, I trust in you." To help me remember, I will tape this verse in a place where I will see it often:

> Trust in the Lord with all your heart,
>   and do not rely on your own insight.
> In all your ways acknowledge him,
>   and he will make straight your paths. (Proverbs 3:5–6)

❧Scriptures for Daily Reflection

This week, begin each daily Scripture reflection time with the "palms down, palms up" prayer (see page 51). Make a special effort to release all anxiety to him. If there is a struggle you are going through, ask him specifically in the "palms up" time to fill you with all the grace you need to persevere through this struggle. If you are not presently in a struggle, praise him for his goodness to you and enjoy his presence.

❧Day One: Fruit of the Spirit

By contrast, the fruit of the Spirit is love, joy, peace, patience, kindness, generosity, faithfulness, gentleness, and self-control. There is no law against such things. (Galatians 5:22–23)

Lord, you possess all of these qualities, and I want to grow to be more like you. Help me to become more patient, kind, gentle, and self-controlled. And help me to appreciate your Spirit's work within me. Here is one area in my life where I especially need a powerful work of the Spirit…

Continue the reflection below:

....

....

....

....

....

....

....

❧ Day Two: Called by Glory

His divine power has given us everything needed for life and
godliness, through the knowledge of him who called us by his
own glory and goodness. (2 Peter 1:3)

You have called me by name, Lord. You have helped me to know you
in a more personal way. And you give me all the grace I need to live out
your call. Thank you. Where are you calling me today, Lord?

Continue the reflection below:

....

....

....

....

....

....

....

....

....

❧ Day Three: Free Indeed

So if the Son makes you free, you will be free indeed. (John 8:36)

Freedom…I would love to be free of all the things in life that weigh me
down, Lord—my moods, my passions, my ambitions, my failings. But

you are teaching me that the most important freedom is the freedom to love you with my whole heart, and others as myself. When I strive to please you and to depend on you for the grace to serve others, I become truly free. How do you want me to experience that freedom today, Lord Jesus?

Continue the reflection below:

....

....

....

....

....

....

....

....

....

....

Day Four: Born of God

But to all who received him, who believed in his name, he gave power to become children of God, who were born, not of blood or of the will of the flesh or of the will of man, but of God. (John 1:12–13)

Lord, I was born to eternal life through my baptism. You received me into your family once and for all. I want to continue to be open to your grace so that I can grow into the fulfilled and joyful spiritual child you always imagined I would be. Lord, how do you want me to live out my baptismal promises today?

Continue the reflection below:

....

....

....

....

....

....

....

....

....

....

✤Day Five: All Things New

And the one who was seated on the throne said, "See, I am making all things new." Also he said, "Write this, for these words are trustworthy and true." (Revelation 21:5)

Lord, practicing virtue is fraught with pitfalls! I fail daily...multiple times each day. Thank goodness that each time I confess my sins, you make "all things new." Shine your light of truth in me, so that I see with full clarity the shadowy areas of my life you most want to transform. Where do you want to begin today, Lord Jesus?

Continue the reflection below:

....
....
....
....
....
....
....
....
....

❦Day Six: Obedience through Suffering

Although he was a Son, he learned obedience through what he
suffered; and having been made perfect, he became the source of
eternal salvation for all who obey him.... (Hebrews 5:8–9)

Lord, you learned obedience through suffering. And what abundant
grace came to all mankind as a result! Help me to remember that when
I suffer while trying to grow in virtue, it glorifies you and reaps eternal
benefits for me and those I love here on earth, and for souls in purga-
tory as well. By your grace, no suffering is ever wasted. Help me to be
especially mindful of this today.

Continue the reflection below:

....
....

....

....

....

....

....

....

....

....

❧*Day Seven: Be Perfect*

For if you love those who love you, what reward do you have?
Do not even the tax collectors do the same? And if you greet only
your brothers and sisters, what more are you doing than others?
Do not even the Gentiles do the same? Be perfect, therefore, as
your heavenly Father is perfect. (Matthew 5:46–48)

Lord, I feel far from perfect! But I am learning what it means to be
mature. I know that many people I meet on a daily basis could benefit
from a smile or a kind word, or by my merely noticing them. I don't
have to add a long list of to-do items to my day in order to love others
with the love you have shown me. By these small gestures, divinely
inspired, you perfect me as I try to do your will.

Continue the reflection below:

....

....

....

On the Winds of Praise

After eating, growing, shedding, cocooning, hatching, stretching, waiting, and strengthening, the mature butterfly finally takes to the air in flight!

Butterflies learn to fly quickly because they need to search for food as soon as possible to fuel their newly active lifestyle. The butterfly is very clever, however, and flies only when the conditions are just right. A rainstorm or gusty wind can prove fatal for the vulnerable, large-winged aeronaut. She knows her limits and, if at all possible, does not fly where or when she will put herself in danger.

* * *

Most butterflies do not migrate, or migrate only short distances. The North American eastern monarch, however, has a most mind-boggling itinerary. This species starts out in Mexico and ends up in Canada! It takes three generations of butterflies, male and female, to reach Canada; each of these generations migrates several hundred miles northward, going through its life cycle in about six weeks.

Something remarkable happens with the next (fourth) generation, however. The fourth-generation butterfly is able to make the flight all the way back from Canada to Mexico! This butterfly lives up to nine months, long enough to navigate to the very place where her ancestors originated several generations prior to her birth. Scientists still do not understand the mystery of why this fourth-generation butterfly is so different, nor how she knows where to return. All fourth-generation monarchs living east of the Rockies fly back to within the same sixty-mile radius in Mexico, no matter where they are coming from across Canada and the northern United States.

Yes, this fourth-generation monarch is a remarkable creature. She is genetically indistinguishable from the three prior generations. Yet in spite of her fragility, she is able to flutter and then use gentle winds to take her where she needs to go. The butterfly is not really designed to fly; rather, she soars like a glider on thermal currents to amazing altitudes—upward of eleven thousand feet (more than two miles). While migrating she can cover more than two hundred miles per day.

Amazingly, upon arrival in Mexico, this fourth-generation

dynamo actually weighs more, in spite of all of her activity, than when she left Canada. Once she arrives, this unbelievable Wonder Woman of a butterfly will rest in the protective branches of a mountainside oyamel fir tree and overwinter for the season, getting plenty of R & R. Her life is not yet over. Come spring, she will once again take to the skies, heading back north!

The illustrious fourth-generation monarch is one blessed among many, though in appearance she looks just like any other butterfly. Her strength, her longevity, and her navigational ability make her a rare breed, indeed. She is truly set apart—yet her giftedness fulfills a purpose. This fourth-generation butterfly reminds us that with great blessings comes great responsibility: "From everyone to whom much has been given, much will be required" (Luke 12:48). She will need to use what God has given her to go far beyond the ordinary.

What gifts has God given you? How can you use your gifts for his purposes? He wants to help you soar higher and farther than perhaps you ever knew that you could. God delights in watching you live up to your potential. Ask him how he would like to use all that he has given to you for his glory and purpose. Is something holding you back? Ask him to show you what it is and to give you the grace to defeat it, and then ask him to give you the courage to take to the sky and soar!

A truly amazing thing about the fourth-generation monarch is how she gets to Mexico. She does not use up all of her energy by trying to get there by her own strength. She glides on the air currents and "rides on the wings of the wind" (Psalm 104:3). We can do the same thing. We can soar on the breath, the *pneuma* of God.[9] Jesus explains: "The wind blows where it chooses, and you hear the sound of it, but you do not know where it comes from or where it goes. So it is with everyone who is born of the Spirit" (John 3:8).

How do we soar like the mature adult butterfly? We must first call upon and be filled with the Holy Spirit.

Come, Holy Spirit, come! Fill me now so that I can do all that you intend for me to do! Help me to be able to soar!

Once we have invited him to fill us to overflowing, we can pray in praise and thanksgiving. In the Old Testament book of Psalms, we read: "The Lord is my strength and my shield; / in him my heart trusts; / so I am helped, and my heart exults; / and with my song I give thanks to him" (Psalm 28:7). And the book of Nehemiah admonishes us, "The joy of the Lord is your strength" (Nehemiah 8:10).

Do you want God to be your strength? Do you want to call heaven down to earth, or better yet call earth up to heaven? Do you want to soar on the breath of God? Then learn how to praise him! We praise him not because things are always perfect and wonderful, but because he is worthy of our praise! And when we get our focus off of our circumstances and onto him, we begin to find strength as his Spirit fills us up and lifts us to new heights. Try it!

❧ Thoughts to Ponder

Take a moment to ponder the following, and journal the thoughts and impressions that arise. If you are taking part in a group study, consider highlighting or marking in the margins points you would like to share with the group.

God lifts our spirits up when we praise him. So where does praise begin? How you feed your mind—what you watch and listen to—can make a big difference in how well disposed you are to praising God. To kick-start your efforts, you might want to try listening to Christian radio during the day. It can turn your heart, your mind, and your gaze heavenward. Or try reading the psalms aloud. There, you will find words to express your desire to praise God. You can also find little prayer books full of written prayers of praise. Or listen closely to the words of the Mass; many of the prayers praise God. Want to go for a walk and be inspired by the outdoors? Let your heart sing to the Lord. Words aren't always necessary! What are some other ways you might turn your heart toward God in praise?

....

....

....

....

....

....

....

....

....

Praise is powerful in times of trouble. As a friend once told me when I was experiencing a rough patch, "Melissa, you are going to have to learn to preach yourself happy!" Wise people learn to focus on the answer rather than the problem by centering their minds, hearts, and souls on God and leaving their problems or circumstances in his capable hands. When we worry that a problem is too *big* for God, it's time for a reality check...and prayers of praise help us see those problems in a new light.

Prayers of praise remind us of who God is—all-powerful, all-capable, all-loving, and completely worthy of our praise! Powerful praises to God are the right answer to any problem. Think of a time when God came through for you, and start to praise him…Go ahead, you can do it!

....

....

....

....

....

....

....

....

....

....

Don't forget to "soar" on the winds of praise! Want to know a little secret? Praising and resting in God go hand in hand. When you praise the Lord, soaring on the breath of the Spirit, you are actually refueling your soul. The Lord is pouring in his grace to overflowing so that, like the butterfly, you actually weigh more—spiritually speaking—than you did when you started.

Just as God gives the fourth-generation monarch the amazing ability to fly all the way from Canada to Mexico, he will give you the strength to do all that he asks of you as well. When we act in accordance with God's will, we discover soon that we are not operating from our own strength, using up our own fuel. We are being fueled by the strength and power of God!

And the soaring monarch has another lesson for us. When she gets to Mexico, she rests after her long journey. We too need times of physical rest. God does not want us to burn out in any way. We must learn not to race ahead or lag behind, but to soar or rest when he nudges us. Can you think of some times when you have especially needed to "rest in God"?

....

....

....

....

....

....

....

....

....

....

A Moment with St. John of the Cross

Let us rejoice, beloved,
And let us go forth to behold ourselves in Your beauty,
To the mountains and to the hill,
To where the pure water flows,
And further, deep into the thicket.[10]
—from "The Spiritual Canticle"

From the "pure waters" to the "thicket," we find sustenance and rest in the loving heart of God. Write about the images that come to mind as you ponder this beautiful stanza from St. John of the Cross. When your soul is weary, where does God invite you to find refreshment?

....

....

....

....

....

....

....

....

....

❧ Thoughts for Discussion

The following questions may be used in a group setting or as additional journaling prompts.

The idea of doing God's will can be scary. The enemy taunts us that if we give God control of our lives, God will force us to do something truly awful. Or we incorrectly assume that when we offer to God what we love most, what he gives in return won't satisfy.

However, the fourth-generation butterfly teaches us the truth about doing God's will: When we comply to the best of our ability, the Lord takes us to new and amazing heights. He blesses us so superabundantly that we experience "the peace of God, which surpasses all understanding" (Philippians 4:7).

• Can you share an experience of divine peace or unexplained strength in the midst of a circumstance that should have been full of challenges, suffering, or sorrow?

....

....

....

....

....

....

....

• Where, by God's grace, do you soar? What would you say are your areas of giftedness? In a spirit of gratitude, share at least one of your God-given gifts. Here is a partial list of gifts to get the discussion rolling: leadership, administration, healing, hospitality, mercy, evangelization, prophecy, music, encouragement...

....

....

....

....

....

....

....

....

• Do you give yourself permission to rest? Believe it or not, resting is part of becoming spiritually mature. It is a bit like putting on our own oxygen mask before helping others. If we are unable to function, we can be of no use to God or to others, as he tells us in the book of Isaiah: "...In returning and rest you shall be saved; / in quietness and in trust shall be your strength..." (Isaiah 30:15). How do you rest and refresh in order to face life's next challenge? God gives us enough strength to do what he asks of us. If you are exhausted all the time, perhaps pray and see if you are doing more than he is asking of you. Discuss the criteria you use to make your to-do list.

....

....

....

....

....

....

....

• What are some of your favorite ways to praise God? Do you listen to praise music? Read the psalms? Keep gratitude journals? Share any experiences you have had with these or any other ways you have learned to lift your eyes and heart heavenward.

....

....

....

....

....

....

....

Let's close with a prayer of praise—perhaps one you have composed yourself! Close your eyes, and turn your palms up, ready to receive the breath of the Spirit as you lift your praises to him.

Prayer

Dear Lord,

Thank you for meeting me right where I am. I praise you for so many blessings in our lives. I praise you for the opportunity to meet with you and learn more about you. I praise you just because you are worthy of praise; as I worship you, I see that you are big, and my problems shrink by comparison.

Go with me now and give me the strength I need to be and to do all that you envision for me. Be with my sisters in faith as well, that we might all learn to soar on your breath, simply by praising and resting in you and allowing you to take us where we need to go. Help us to spread our wings and soar with you this week.

I ask this in the name of the Father, the Son, and the Holy Spirit. Amen.

A "Renewing Truth"

Every time I go in or out of my door I will say,

"I praise you, God, for _____. Your Word says, 'The joy of the Lord is [my] strength'!" (Nehemiah 8:10).

✹ *Scriptures for Daily Reflection*

This week, along with reading the Scripture verses and doing the "palms down, palms up" prayer, incorporate one of these praise exercises each day:

- Dance! *When your feet first hit the floor in the morning, dance around and get your day started off on a happy note.*
- Smile at Jesus. *If you can't make it to Adoration (which is a very good thing to do), ask Jesus to sit with you for a few moments right where you are. Close your eyes, and imagine him sitting right next to you, smiling at you. Don't forget to smile back!*
- Sing a new song to Jesus. *Make up a tune to your favorite Bible verse or quote and sing it to the Lord.*
- Take a nap. *Right in the middle of the day. Even if you have a thousand things to do. Just twenty minutes. Revel in how good it feels, and praise the Lord!*

✹ *Day One: I Praise You*

I will extol you, my God and King,
  and bless your name for ever and ever.
Every day I will bless you,
  and praise your name for ever and ever.
Great is the LORD, and greatly to be praised;
  his greatness is unsearchable.

One generation shall laud your works to another,
  and shall declare your mighty acts.
On the glorious splendor of your majesty,
  and on your wondrous works, I will meditate.
The might of your awesome deeds shall be proclaimed,
  and I will declare your greatness.

They shall celebrate the fame of your abundant goodness,
and shall sing aloud of your righteousness. (Psalm 145:1–7)

Lord, teach me to praise you. I want to praise you when my heart is overflowing with joy, and also when I'm not so happy, because I know very well that you are deserving of my praise. Here are just a few of the reasons why…

Continue the reflection below:

....

....

....

....

....

....

....

....

....

Day Two: Bless the Lord

Bless the LORD, O my soul,
and do not forget all his benefits—
who forgives all your iniquity,
who heals all your diseases,

…

who satisfies you with good as long as you live
so that your youth is renewed like the eagle's. (Psalm 103:2–3, 5)

Lord, you do many, many good things for me each day. I am so grateful. Inspire me this day to live out my gratitude to you in a small, concrete way for all the many benefits you bring into my life, such as…

Continue the reflection below:

....

....

....

....

....

....

....

....

....

....

✤ Day Three: Enter with Thanksgiving

Enter his gates with thanksgiving,

and his courts with praise.

Give thanks to him, bless his name. (Psalm 100:4)

I never have to look too hard to find ways to praise you, Lord. The Scriptures, especially the Psalms, give me the words I seek. Your "gates" and "courts" remind me of coming into church for Mass. I will whisper a word of praise to you every time I kneel down and each time I hear your Word proclaimed. Let me praise you for your faithfulness as did Mary and the apostles and all the saints!

Continue the reflection below:

....

....

....

....

....

....

....

....

....

....

❧Day Four: You Created All Things

You are worthy, our Lord and God,
  to receive glory and honor and power,
for you created all things,
  and by your will they existed and were created. (Revelation 4:11)

A special way to praise you is by appreciating your works in nature, Lord. When I see a beautiful sunset, or feel the warmth of sun on my face, or notice raindrops on a blooming flower, or hear birds chirp on spring mornings, I think of you, my Creator. How wonderful are your works! Even now I look outside and see...

Continue the reflection below:

....

....
....
....
....
....
....
....
....

✤ Day Five: Renew My Strength

But those who wait for the LORD shall renew their strength,

they shall mount up with wings like eagles,

they shall run and not be weary,

they shall walk and not faint. (Isaiah 40:31)

Lord, I need your strength! I can imagine the butterfly gliding care-free on the wind, but my feet stay firmly planted on the ground. My heavy heart keeps me from soaring, and my legs feel so tired. One day, however, the earth will release its hold on me and I will *soar* into your arms, Lord. Thank you for creating me for heaven, and keep me safe while I sojourn here.

Continue the reflection below:

....
....
....

....

....

....

....

....

....

....

❧*Day Six: Spiritual Gifts*

Now concerning spiritual gifts, brothers and sisters, I do not want you to be uninformed. (1 Corinthians 12:1)

Lord, everyone has at least one spiritual gift, right? Help me see myself the way you see me, with the gifts you intend for me to use. I want to appreciate every gift you have given me, and to use them all for your glory and the benefit of others. What dormant gifts do I have laying within me, Lord? Show me, as you see fit. I want to do what you want me to do with my life.

Continue the reflection below:

....

....

....

....

....

....

....

....

....

....

❧ Day Seven: Rest on the Seventh Day

And on the seventh day God finished the work that he had done, and he rested on the seventh day from all the work that he had done. (Genesis 2:2)

Lord, you rested on the seventh day, and I am called to imitate you. Every Sunday is meant to be a respite from daily life. Show me how to observe the Sabbath rest according to your will, Lord. Help me to find ways to rest so that I am truly refreshed—spiritually, emotionally, and physically. I praise you for answering this simple prayer.

Continue the reflection below:

....

....

....

....

....

....

....

....

Spreading God's Love

As we wrap up our six weeks of reflection on the monarch butterfly, a little review is in order.

In session one we learned that we are uniquely and lovingly made to love and to be loved. The Creator longs to transform us from something small and seemingly insignificant, like a minuscule butterfly egg, into a beautiful, spiritually mature child of God, like the regal monarch.

In session two, we discovered that we are what we eat! Our path to maturation involves learning to eat what is good for us and to avoid what is not. We explored the sacrament of the Eucharist as our true soul food and the sacrament of reconciliation as cleansing us of all harmful "soul toxins."

In session three, we looked at how to "cocoon" with God. We don't try to do his will with our own strength. We isolate ourselves, quiet our hearts, and learn to hear his voice speaking into our busy lives! It is by cocooning that we allow ourselves to be remade, strengthened, and emboldened to live large!

In session four, we discovered the importance of emerging from prayer time each day in order to stretch our wings and practice virtues—good habits—which lead to balance, peace, moderation, and a host of other desirable qualities. By God's grace, in concert with our efforts, we are being transformed and made more spiritually beautiful!

In session five, we found that as we practice these spiritual habits, our "wings" grow strong, and before we know it we are soaring on the power of the Holy Spirit! We can find ourselves in the midst of everyday trials—traffic jams, unwelcome chores, fractious relationships—with a soul animated by the praise of God and saturated in the "peace that surpasses all understanding."

In this last session, we will examine another important phase in the life of the monarch, in which life is passed on to the next generation. This is the natural part of a healthy life cycle: life begets life. As we will discover, this principle is true in the spiritual realm as well....

Today we come to the last phase of the monarch butterfly's life cycle. It is hard to believe that, in spite of its complexity, a butterfly's life span is actually very short. Most monarchs live only two to six weeks after hatching from their chrysalis. Think about it: they live only as long as it takes to get through this study.

The exception, of course, is the fourth-generation monarch, which we discussed in session five. She is a very unique creature indeed. But after she has flown all the way back to Mexico and wintered high up in the oyamel fir trees of the Reserva de la Biosfera Mariposa Monarca (Monarch Butterfly Biosphere Reserve), she awakens and starts the first leg of the trek northward, instinctively heading toward Canada, just as her parents and ancestors did before her.

The mature butterfly starts out looking for only two things: food and a mate. Because most butterflies live so briefly, they are extremely intent on reproducing. Adult monarchs are very busy. One female butterfly can lay up to five hundred eggs, one at a time, on many different milkweed leaves so that their hatchlings will not have to travel for a tasty meal. They simply hatch and eat, naturally protected from predators.

Although the butterfly may not know it, she has another important job beyond her own agenda of eating and reproducing. Butterflies are great pollinators! The butterfly's wings, feet, and other body parts brush up against flowers as she goes about her daily business. She helps to stir up and distribute the pollen necessary for flower and fruit production. In her very beautiful and peculiar way, she kicks up blossom dander for a most unusual reason—she wants to find out if the flower will be nutritious, and she tastes with her feet! While doing so, she leaves a trail of very happy blooms behind her; and in return, the flowers offer their life-sustaining nectar as nourishment.

- -

The mature butterfly seems to be in a hurry to eat and reproduce—to live life to the fullest. We should be as well. Our lives are short, and as much as we do not want to think about it, we are all at some point going to die. Knowing that we only have a finite number of spins on this planet, we should greatly appreciate what we have been given and use it all for the glory of the One who gave it to us. That calls for living with intensity and purpose.

Living with intensity means making an effort to get to know the One with whom we will hopefully spend all of eternity, our Butterfly Father—the One who makes life truly worth living. We do this, as we have discussed, by meeting God every morning for a quiet time of prayer to share our needs, to ask his blessing on those we love, and to receive his grace and friendship.

Living with purpose means recognizing, like the female monarch, that we have a mission, and doing our best to fulfill God's will for us. The female butterfly is loaded with life and needs to deposit it. Do you know that you too are pregnant with "life"? If we humbly say yes to God as Mary did, and allow the Holy Spirit to fill us, we in a sense bear Christ to the world as Mary did. That is how we are able to reproduce spiritual life all around us.

Are you desperate to lay eggs of love in as many places as possible? We "reproduce" God's love every time we do something in his strength and for him. Each and every daily task at home, at work, or at play, no matter how small or insignificant, can be a deposit of love—a little prayer—if it's offered to God. We can be in a state of constant prayer, doing our very best for his honor and glory. And we just never know what will hatch from our lovingly made deposits. Love begets love.

The butterfly pollinates as a natural part of her daily life. So should we. The Bible tells us that we are called to "make disciples" (Matthew 28:19); we do so by bringing the love of Christ to whomever we meet, wherever we go. We engage and connect with others, sharing the love we ourselves have experienced. It comes naturally when we're full of the Holy Spirit. It is a true mark of spiritual maturity to "kick up the dust" of the Spirit, sharing it as we go from place to place and leaving behind us a trail of happy souls.

After six weeks of meeting with God daily, you have likely experienced some changes in your life...perhaps more love, joy, peace, patience, kindness, generosity, faithfulness, gentleness, or self-control (see Galatians 5:22)? These are the fruits of the Holy Spirit, as distinctive as the marks of a mature imago-stage butterfly. When you cocoon with your Heavenly Father, he shares these fruits with you as he fills you with his Holy Spirit. He shares these gifts with you so that you can graciously, freely, lovingly, and generously share these gifts with others—so that they too can be transformed and made new.

God bless you, and thank you for taking this journey with me. May you truly know that you are deeply, completely, and wholly loved by our Butterfly Father. And may his love cause you to be transformed by grace, so that you always and everywhere desire union with him because...

YOU WERE BORN TO SOAR!

❧ *Thoughts to Ponder*

Take a moment to ponder the following, and journal the thoughts and impressions that arise. If you are taking part in a group study, consider highlighting or marking in the margins points you would like to share with the group.

Do little things with great love. This phrase summarizes St. Thérèse of Lisieux's "Little Way" of holiness. Like Mary, we are called to nurture our relationship with Christ, whom we carry within our hearts, through the indwelling of the Holy Spirit. What little sacrifice or hidden act of service could you offer to the Lord today? Tomorrow? Every day?

....

....

....

....

....

One way of pleasing God is to pray for others. Think about how or when you might do this, and write a few prayer goals in the space below. Keep it simple and sustainable. Would you prefer to pray at church? At home? At night before bedtime? If you have a prayer journal, do you go back and make note of answered prayers and thank God for them? Do you have any other ideas about how to pray for others or develop the habit of praying for others?

Make a list below (not to be shared!) of people who need your prayers (perhaps include the person you find most difficult to love), and ask the Lord for the strength to commit to praying or sacrificing for them.

....

....

....

....

....

....

....

....

....

....

....

....

Spend your time well. Most monarch butterflies live six short weeks or less. By comparison, we live much, much longer. And yet our earthly lives are but a fraction of a second in the context of eternity.

Are you spending your time well—as a Christ bearer to friends and neighbors? Are you active in your local parish, both for your own spiritual growth and to help others along the way? What kind of outreach do you find yourself doing most naturally? (Do you like to invite friends to church with you? Take food to friends in need, or serve in a soup kitchen?) Have you thought about sharing this study with friends? Examine your gifts, and ask God what he would have you do.

....

....

....

....

....

....

....

....

....

....

❧A Moment with St. John of the Cross

The breathing of the air,
The song of the sweet nightingale
The grove and its living beauty
In the serene night,
With a flame that is consuming and painless.[11]
—from "The Spiritual Canticle"

The words of St. John of the Cross speak of the simplicity and joy of a fruitful encounter with God. Being with God doesn't need to be complicated; it doesn't require your knowing just the right words. It is as simple and natural as breathing, as acknowledging the longing to receive all God wants to give. What do you most long to receive from God today?

❧ *Thoughts for Discussion*

The following questions may be used in a group setting or as additional journaling prompts.

St. Peter says, "Always be ready to make your defense to anyone who demands from you an accounting for the hope that is in you; yet do it with gentleness and reverence...." (1 Peter 3:15–16). Take a few minutes to write your own story. Don't make it complicated or long—just write about what you've experienced (maybe newly during this past six weeks). Jot down a few paragraphs, enough to be able to convey your story in two to three minutes. Here are a few questions to consider as you write.

• What changes have you felt or seen as you have grown in your relationship with God? What difference does knowing Christ make in your life?

• How would you describe your experience of this study, during which you sought to encounter Christ daily through prayer?

....

....

....

....

....

....

....

....

• What was your life like before encountering God in a real and personal way? How it is different now?

....

....

....

....

....

....

....

....

....

• Imagine someone asking you why you go to church or pray or believe in Jesus. What would you say? How has your faith made a difference in your life?

....

....

....

....

....

....

....

You never know—you may have an opportunity to share your story sometime soon. So be prepared, be bold, and spread the love of God that you have received wherever you go!

My story:

....

....

....

....

....

....

....

....

....

If you are using this journal as part of a prayer group, have the group break into pairs before you close in prayer so that each person has an opportunity to share what she has written.

Prayer

Dear Lord,

Thank you for meeting me right where I am. Thank you for giving me more of you, so that I can share my story with others. Let my heart be so full of love for you that people will notice: "What's up? You seem so at peace!" Take my heart and set it on fire with love for you, so that I can't help but share with others all that you have done for me. Lift me up to soar closer and closer to your beautiful heart of love. Help me to experience what it means to be truly in union with you and with all those who love you.

I ask this in the name of the Father, the Son, and the Holy Spirit. Amen.

A "Renewing Truth"

Every time I do [the laundry, the dishes, something I don't really like doing], I will do it humbly, offering it up as an act of love for God and allowing him to transform it into a "reproductive" act. I will repeat in my mind:

> Love is patient; love is kind.... It bears all things, believes all things, hopes all things, endures all things. (1 Corinthians 13:4, 7)

Scriptures for Daily Reflection

I want to thank you once more for coming along on this journey with me. God is eternal, and we can never come to the end of him. Therefore,

I pray that you will continue to "cocoon" with him daily and emerge anew, refreshed and ready to soar as you grow closer and closer to him with each new metamorphosis! You will see that the more you cocoon, the easier it will be. May you be greatly blessed as you abandon yourself to the ways and love of God.

❦ Day One: Competence from God

Such is the confidence that we have through Christ toward God. Not that we are competent of ourselves to claim anything as coming from us; our competence is from God. (2 Corinthians 3:4–5)

Holy Spirit, you initiate within me every good thing I am able to do for others. When I feel like I am "making progress" or "getting a lot done" or "listening well," remind me that you are there within me, inspiring and guiding me. Help me to rest in you and rely on your strength!

Continue the reflection below:

....

....

....

....

....

....

....

....

....

....

❧ Day Two: With All Your Heart

"You shall love the Lord your God with all your heart, and with all your soul, and with all your mind." This is the greatest and the first commandment. And a second is like it: "You shall love your neighbor as yourself." (Matthew 22:37–39)

Lord Jesus, you call me to love you completely, but I don't know how! Show me what delights you, so that I can love you better and more. Help me to realize, with your grace, what I'm good at and how to help others with these gifts you have uniquely given to me.

Continue the reflection below:

....

....

....

....

....

....

....

....

....

....

❧ Day Three: Heavenly Reward

Beware of practicing your piety before others in order to be seen by them; for then you have no reward from your Father in heaven. (Matthew 6:1)

Thank you, Lord, for this helpful reminder. When I am about your work—spreading your word, being your hands, your feet, your voice—all the glory belongs to you and you alone! When people come in contact with me, let them come away with the sense that they have met you today. Please especially strengthen me to show your love when I find it hardest to do…

Continue the reflection below:

....

....

....

....

....

....

....

....

....

....

Day Four: Peace Be with You

Jesus said to them again, "Peace be with you. As the Father has sent me, so I send you." (John 20:21)

Lord Jesus, sometimes it's hard to be faithful to my call as a Christian! The littlest things can seem so difficult. I hesitate to stand out or speak up. Remind me, Lord, that you are with me and that you promise your peace! Help me to recognize your presence in every difficult situation of my life…

Continue the reflection below:

....

....

....

....

....

....

....

....

....

....

❧ Day Five: A Future with Hope

For surely I know the plans I have for you, says the Lord, plans
for your welfare and not for harm, to give you a future with
hope. (Jeremiah 29:11)

Lord, what a beautiful promise you give me in this verse of Scripture to
remind me that you see the big picture. When life is tough, I need hope,
and you remind me here that you've got my back, that you want only
my good. You are completely trustworthy, even when I do not understand your plan. Praise to you, Lord Jesus Christ!

Continue the reflection below:

....

....

....

....

....

....

....

....

....

....

❧*Day Six: I Am with You Always*

And Jesus came and said to them, "All authority in heaven and on earth has been given to me. Go therefore and make disciples of all nations, baptizing them in the name of the Father and of the Son and of the Holy Spirit, and teaching them to obey everything that I have commanded you. And remember, I am with you always, to the end of the age." (Matthew 28:18–20)

Lord Jesus, you love me intimately and personally, knowing my weaknesses and strengths—just as you knew those you sent out into the world to proclaim your message. Help me to take up the task you have given me to do, no matter how challenging it seems. Strengthen me with your love, and guide me where you want me to go, confident in your authority as my God and Creator. Help me to use the gifts you have given me; inspire me to carry out your directive to "go…and make disciples." I know you will accompany me and never leave me alone!

Continue the reflection below:

....
....
....
....
....
....
....
....

Day Seven: By My Spirit

...Not by might, nor by power, but by my spirit, says the LORD of hosts. (Zechariah 4:6)

It can be easy to look at the world around me and become afraid of speaking and acting on the truth, Lord. And yet your Spirit, while gentle, kind, and good, is also powerful, raising up the lowly and making us fearless. Send your Spirit to me today in a new and fresh way. Let me never be afraid to soar!

Continue the reflection below:

....
....
....
....

Magis: Doing Something Greater for God

Magis (pronounced MAH-gis) is a Latin word that means "more" or "better." It refers to the philosophy of doing more for Christ—*ad majorem Dei gloriam* ("for the greater glory of God," which is at the heart of Jesuit spirituality)

Do you want to do something for others, for the greater glory of God? Get your group together in the next week and reach out to share with others the love you have received.

Start by thinking about the needs of your immediate community, especially your parish; check with your pastor for ideas. Or reach out to those in need in your city. There are many ways you can help. Once you've decided on a project, be sure to invite a friend or two to come along.

Some suggestions: beautify the parish grounds by planting flowers or raking leaves; bring supplies to a local shelter; serve food to the homeless; volunteer at a food pantry; deliver diapers to a crisis pregnancy center.

But don't forget to keep feeding on the Eucharist and the Word and strengthening your "wings" by growing in virtue. Above all, don't forget to spend time "cocooning" with God. Unlike the monarch, we need that time alone with God every day of our lives! In the following pages, you will find some more ideas for how to "cocoon" with God.

More Ways to "Cocoon" with God

1. Practice *lectio divina* (divine reading).

This is what we have been doing during our study—now take it up a notch. Using a parish missal or an online resource, read through the daily Mass readings slowly.[12] Notice which one or two lines speak to you from each reading, and write one or two sentences to God about those lines in your journal. Spend special time on the Gospel reading; in order to encounter Christ, it is important to spend time pondering the life and teachings of Jesus.

2. Go to daily Mass.

Check local Mass schedules at www.masstimes.org or in your parish bulletin (which can often be found online). Be sure to arrive a few minutes early, and ask God to open your heart and speak to you. If your parish does not offer daily Mass at a time you can easily attend, be sure to spend time in Eucharistic Adoration. Jesus is waiting there in the tabernacle to connect with you!

3. Pray using the ACTS model.

Just as we spend time talking with people in order to get to know them better, so we need to spend time with God every day if we want our relationship with him to grow deeper. Conversation with God is a two-way street. It is important to tell God what is on our hearts and then to *listen* to the quiet words he speaks to us in our hearts. This two-way conversation can be summarized by the acronym ACTS (Adoration, Contrition, Thanksgiving, Supplication).

Adoration: Begin by putting yourself quietly in the presence of God. Turn your attention fully to being with him, opening your heart to receive his love. Adore God. Recall his attributes: almighty, powerful, omnipresent. Read a psalm of praise and thanksgiving. Sing a song of praise.

Contrition: Have you done or said anything that you now regret? Confess whatever sins the Holy Spirit brings to mind. If you feel "stuck" in sin, or believe that your sins have created a distance between you and God, there is hope! You can experience his forgiveness in the sacrament of reconciliation. Make note and go as soon as possible. (Don't forget that the Eucharist can also forgive less serious sins and strengthen us against falling back into sinful habits—*CCC* 1394.)

Thanksgiving: Thank God for all he has given to you. Name your blessings and answered prayers. Cultivate an "attitude of gladitude"! This will bolster your faith to ask more of him. (Did you know that the word *Eucharist* means "thanksgiving"?)

Supplication: What do you need most from God? Don't be afraid to ask God to supply your needs and the needs of those around you. Intercede for others, and share your concerns with him.

4. Cultivate the habit of spiritual reading.

Go to your parish library or local bookstore and feed your mind on spiritually uplifting "soul food." If you enjoyed the poetry of St. John of the Cross, consider reading more of his work—or find a copy of St. Teresa of Avila's *Interior Castle.* If you're looking for something you can easily pick up and put down, consider familiarizing yourself with the Divine Office (the daily prayers of the Church), or choose a small prayer book such as *Hearts on Fire: Praying with Jesuits* by Michael Harter, SJ, or *The*

Catholic Prayer Book by Monsignor Michael Buckley. Another book I have found very helpful is *Miracle Hour* by Linda Schubert.

5. Keep journaling!

Get yourself a beautifully bound journal with blank pages inside in which to record your thoughts and prayers as you continue to read Scripture and invite the Holy Spirit to speak to you though its pages. Ask yourself: "How can I love you, Lord, more today than I did yesterday?"

6. Sing praise and worship music.

Turn your heart and mind to heaven by listening to Christian music on CDs or your local Catholic or Christian radio station.

7. Consider seeking spiritual direction.

A good spiritual director will help you to learn to connect to God (cocoon) and to discern what God is telling you when you do. If you are unsure how to find a good spiritual director, contact your pastor or diocesan office. You might also visit a local retreat house or go online to Spiritual Directors International (www.sdiworld.org).

What the caterpillar calls the end of the world,
the master calls a butterfly.

—Richard Bach

ACKNOWLEDGMENTS

A very special thanks to Servant and Franciscan Media for believing in me, especially my editor, Heidi Saxton, who is a brilliant servant of God.

And to the first Born to Soar small group. Leaders: Katelin Haney and Annie Sabel, whose love, encouragement, and input were invaluable. Participants: Barbara Applebee, Amy Baier, Philippa Bender, Kristin Cecchi, Holly Geist, Katie Gormley, Lanie Mann, Christie Pell Neal, Vita Pagnani, Mary Margaret Plumridge, Jayda Reid, Sara Sigrist, and Nancy Zoa-Finn, all of who helped to give wings to this study.

Tips for Small-Group Leaders

Once you have done this study on your own (either using the journal alone or with the video component offered through www.FranciscanMedia.org), you may decide you would like to invite a few friends to do the study with you! If this is your first experience as a small-group leader, congratulations! You do not need to be a Bible scholar or trained theologian to lead a small-group study. All you need is a love for Jesus and a love for other people! But here are a few tips to keep in mind as you prepare to lead your small group through *Born to Soar*.

RUNNING THE MEETINGS

Born to Soar is a personal study that may be used in a small-group setting. The first thing you will need to decide is when and where to hold the meetings. You will also need to decide whether each member will buy her own journal or you will get them for the whole group. (You can order them easily, along with the online video component, through www.FranciscanMedia.org.)

You can hold the meetings in your living room or a small meeting room, almost anywhere a group of people can sit comfortably and see both the screen (for the video component) and one another. You may want to provide light refreshments, at least for the first meeting. Be sure to send out a reminder about the time and place of the meetings a couple of days beforehand, and again the morning of the meeting. Consider placing an announcement in your parish bulletin.

After a brief social time, start each session with a short prayer, followed by the video. At the end of the video, begin the conversation with a few remarks about what you thought about the teaching on the video. Invite others to share as well. Then ask a group member to read aloud the first question from the "Thoughts for Discussion" section. If no one volunteers, you can do the reading until people feel more comfortable.

Answer the "Thoughts for Discussion" questions as a group, allowing time for each person to share if she would like to. It may be helpful for you to share first, since you will have read the materials ahead of time and will have had time to formulate your answers. I pray that you will be thoughtful as well as vulnerable with your answers, as this will help to inspire your group to share honestly and boldly.

If you find that most people have not read the introductory material and "Thoughts to Ponder" sections for each lesson, you may choose to read those aloud. Close each session with the "Prayer" following the "Thoughts for Discussion."

Following Up at Home

While there is no "homework" required in this study, those who would like to learn more about how to connect with God will want to read and journal about the daily Scripture verses found at the end of each session—one per day. After reading the verse and the short reflection, participants can take a few minutes to journal their thoughts and prayers to God in the space provided.

Each session also includes a feature called "A 'Renewing Truth,'" a short Scripture phrase and practice that focuses on the theme of that session. Copies of these weekly verses are included in appendix four, so that they can be cut out and placed on mirrors or in pockets as gentle reminders to keep renewing our thinking and to keep praying and reading Scripture. St. Paul exhorts us:

> Finally, beloved, whatever is true, whatever is honorable, whatever is just, whatever is pure, whatever is pleasing, whatever is commendable, if there is any excellence and if there is anything worthy of praise, think about these things. (Philippians 4:8)

God tells us in his Holy Word that if we want to have peaceful, joyful lives, we should let our minds dwell with him. I hope these little "memory joggers" will help to bring you and the members of your group closer to union with him.

The Sacrament of Reconciliation

WHAT IS THE SACRAMENT OF RECONCILIATION?

Reconciliation (also known as confession or penance) is a sacrament of healing, a way that Jesus Christ, in his love and mercy, provides for us to experience forgiveness whenever we commit an offense against God and other people (see *CCC* 1422–1424). Through confession, we are also reconciled with the Church because our sins create division and disunity that only Jesus can heal (see *CCC* 1443–1445).

Every time we sin, we hurt ourselves, other people, and God. In reconciliation, we acknowledge our sins before God and his Church. We express our sorrow in a meaningful way, receive the forgiveness of Christ and his Church, make reparation for what we have done, and resolve to do better in the future.

The forgiveness of sins involves four parts:

1. Contrition—sincere sorrow for having offended God. This is the most important act of the penitent. Forgiveness is not possible if we are not sorry for what we have done, or if we refuse to resolve not to repeat our sin (see *CCC* 1451–1454).

2. Confession—recounting our sins to God directly and personally, through the ministry of the priest (see *CCC* 1441–1442, 1461–1462). This audible confession encourages true interior repentance and conversion.

3. Absolution—the words spoken by the priest through which God, the Father of Mercies, reconciles a sinner to himself through the merits of the cross (see *CCC* 1449).

4. Penance—the act of reparation the priest imposes in satisfaction for our sins. This is an important part of our healing. "The sinner must still recover his full spiritual health by doing something more to make amends for the sin: He must 'make satisfaction' for…his sins. This satisfaction is also called 'penance'" (*CCC* 1459).

Nervous about Going to Confession?

Whether this is your first confession or you have simply been away for a long time, know that you do not need to be anxious about doing or saying the wrong thing! In confession the priest stands in for Jesus himself and is waiting to welcome you—even if you have been away from the Church for a long, long time. (The sacrament of reconciliation is for those who have been baptized Catholic or are in full communion with the Church. If you are not yet Catholic, most priests will be happy to make an appointment with you to discuss how you might begin the discernment process.)

Just as we do not worry about telling the doctor our symptoms, so we can speak freely to the priest about anything that is troubling us, especially anything we know is creating distance between us and God. In the Gospel of Luke, we read the words of Jesus: "There will be more joy in heaven over one sinner who repents than over ninety-nine righteous persons who need no repentance" (Luke 15:7).

So…let's begin! You can find out when this sacrament is being offered in your parish bulletin; or if you would like a little extra time, just make an appointment with the pastor. Before you go, you may wish to make an "examination of conscience" to help you prepare for the sacrament. Several forms of this reflection are available on the website of the United States Council of Catholic Bishops (www.usccb.org) or other websites,[13] or you can refer to "How to Make an Examination of Conscience" at the end of this appendix.

On the other hand, if there is a particular burden you are carrying and need to confess, simply ask the Lord to give you the words and the courage to say what you need to during the sacrament. (Be honest! Let the Great Physician pour out healing on your deepest and most painful wounds, and experience true freedom from the past!)

When you are making your confession, tell the priest the specific kind of sins you have committed and, to the best of your ability, how many times you have committed them since your last good confession. Avoid generalizations, and inform the priest of any relevant circumstances in which your sins were committed. Always tell the priest your state of life: married or single, priest or religious, or under religious vows or promises.

Although you are obliged to confess only mortal (grave) sins, confession of venial (less serious) sins is very helpful for avoiding sin and advancing in holiness. If you are in doubt about whether a sin is mortal or venial, mention your doubt to the priest. According to the *Catechism*, "For a *sin* to be *mortal*, three conditions must together be met: 'Mortal sin is sin whose object is grave matter and which is also committed with full knowledge and deliberate consent'" (*CCC* 1857).

How to Go to Confession

1. Go behind the screen, or sit in the chair opposite the priest for a face-to-face confession. The priest gives a blessing or greeting.
2. Make the Sign of the Cross and say, "Bless me, Father, for I have sinned. My last confession was [give weeks, months, or years] ago."
3. Confess all your sins to the priest. (If you are unsure or uneasy, tell him and ask for help.)

4. Say, "I am sorry for these and all of my sins."

5. The priest assigns a penance and offers advice to help you avoid future sin and to grow in virtue.

6. Say an Act of Contrition (below), expressing your sorrow for your sins.

7. The priest, acting in the person of Christ, absolves you from your sins.

8. After you leave the confessional, be sure to "make satisfaction" by following through on the priest's instructions for penance. It is part of the sacrament.

An Act of Contrition

O My God, I am sorry for my sins with all my heart. In choosing to do wrong and failing to do good, I have sinned against you, whom I should love above all things. I firmly intend, with the help of your grace, to do penance, to sin no more, and to avoid whatever leads me to sin. Our Savior, Jesus Christ, suffered and died for us. In his name, O Lord, have mercy.

How to Make an Examination of Conscience[14]

An examination of conscience is a prayerful reflection about one's own life and conduct in light of the Ten Commandments and the example and teachings of Christ. Especially when we are weighed down with habitual or serious sin, we need to bring these things to the confessional so that we can receive the healing and support we need to get back on the right path. (Those who have serious sin on their consciences may not receive the Eucharist until they have received the sacrament of reconciliation. When in doubt, go to confession so you can receive all the graces God wants to give you!)

To begin your examination of conscience, ask the Holy Spirit to help you to review your conduct. The steps below, organized by commandment, should assist you in making a thorough, prayerful review:

First Commandment: "I am the Lord your God. You shall have no other gods before me" (Exodus 20:2–3).

• Do I really love God more than anything else this world has to offer? Or have I put other things—work, money, TV, fame, pleasure, other people—ahead of him?

• Do I make time for God each day in prayer?

• Have I dabbled in the occult, or read materials or watched programs that are opposed to faith and morals?

• Do I wholeheartedly accept and follow God's teaching, or do I only pick and choose the convenient parts of his message? Have I tried to learn and understand my faith better?

• Have I denied my faith before others? Have I ever been unwilling to affirm, defend, and practice my faith in public?

• Do I doubt God's mercy for me on one hand, or take advantage of (presume upon) it on the other?

Second Commandment: "You shall not make wrongful use of the name of the Lord your God" (Exodus 20:7).

• Do I love God's name and refrain from saying (or listening to others say) it carelessly or irreverently?

• Have I offended God by blaspheming or cursing?

• Do I try my best to fulfill the promises and resolutions that I have made to God, especially those of my baptism and confirmation?

• Have I shown disrespect for the Blessed Virgin Mary, the saints, the Church, holy things, or holy people?

Third Commandment: "Remember the sabbath day, and keep it holy" (Exodus 20:8).

• Have I deliberately and without serious reason missed Mass on Sunday or on holy days of obligation?

• Have I fully, consciously, and actively participated in Holy Mass, or have I been just going through the motions?

• Have I given my full attention to the Word of God, or have I given in easily to distractions?

• Have I arrived at Mass late due to carelessness?

• Have I left early without a serious reason?

• Have I kept the Eucharistic fast (one hour) before Holy Mass?

• Have I received Holy Communion in a state of mortal sin?

• Did I do work on Sunday that was not necessary?

• Have I used Sunday as just part of the "weekend," or as a day for acts of love toward God, my family, and those in need?

Fourth Commandment: "Honor your father and your mother" (Exodus 20:12).

• Have I neglected my duties to my husband, wife, children, parents, or siblings?

• Have I been ungrateful for the sacrifices my parents made for me?

• Have I disrespected my family members, treated them with scant affection, or reacted proudly when corrected by them?

• Have I caused tension and fights in my family?

• Have I cared for my aged and infirm relatives?

• Have I provided for the Christian education of my children through Catholic school or religious instruction? Do I inspire them by my virtue or scandalize them by my failings?

• When I have disciplined my children, did I do so with charity and prudence?

• Have I encouraged my children to pray about why God created them and whether God may be calling them to the priesthood or religious life?

Fifth Commandment: "You shall not murder" (Exodus 20:13).
- Have I physically harmed anyone?
- Have I attempted suicide or entertained thoughts of taking my own life?
- Have I had an abortion or encouraged or helped someone else to have one? Have I participated in the practice of abortion through my silence, financial support for persons or organizations that promote it, or voting without a very serious reason for candidates who support it?
- Have I taken part in or supported so-called mercy killing (euthanasia)?
- Have I abused my children or others in any way?
- Have I mutilated or harmed my body?
- Have I borne hatred or withheld forgiveness?
- Have I been reckless behind the wheel and put my and others' lives in danger?
- Have I neglected my health?
- Did I set a bad example through drug abuse, drinking alcohol to excess, fighting, or quarreling?
- Have I gotten angry easily or lost my temper?

Sixth & Ninth Commandments: "You shall not commit adultery" (Exodus 20:14). "You shall not covet your neighbor's wife" (Exodus 20:17).
- Have I treated my body as a temple of the Holy Spirit?
- Have I willfully entertained impure thoughts or desires?
- Have I deliberately look at impure TV programs, websites, videos, pictures, or movies?
- Have I committed impure acts with myself (masturbation) or with others through adultery (sex with a married person), fornication (premarital sex), or homosexual activity?

- Have I been faithful to my husband or wife in my heart and in my conduct with others?
- Have I sinned through the use of contraception, contraceptive sterilization, or in vitro fertilization?
- Have I touched or kissed another person in a lustful way?
- Have I treated others, in my deeds or thoughts, as objects?
- Have I been an occasion of sin for others by acting or dressing immodestly?
- Am I married according to the laws of the Church?
- Did I advise or encourage anyone to marry outside the Church?

Seventh & Tenth Commandments: "You shall not steal" (Exodus 20:15). "You shall not covet anything that belongs to your neighbor" (Exodus 20:17).

- Have I been greedy or envious? Have I made acquiring material possessions the focus of my life?
- Am I inordinately attached to the things of this world?
- Did I steal, cheat, or keep stolen goods, or encourage others to steal or keep stolen goods? Have I returned or made restitution for things I have stolen?
- Have I damaged others' property without acknowledging it and repairing it?
- Have I paid my debts, or have I played the system so as to avoid fulfilling my obligations?
- Have I cheated my company? Have I given a full day's work for a full day's pay?
- Have I paid a fair wage to anyone who works for me?
- Have I been faithful to my promises and contracts? Have I given or accepted bribes?
- Have I allowed work to get in the way of my obligations to God or to my family?

- Do I generously share my goods with the needy?
- Am I generous to the work of the Church? Do I share my time, talents, and treasure in the apostolic and charitable works of the Church and in the life of my parish?

Eighth Commandment: "You shall not bear false witness against your neighbor" (Exodus 20:16).
- Have I caused spiritual or material harm to others through lying?
- Have I deliberately told lies about anybody (calumny)?
- Have I injured others by revealing true hidden faults (detraction)?
- Did I commit perjury? Have I been guilty of refusing to testify to the innocence of another because of fear or selfishness?
- Have I engaged in uncharitable talk or gossip?
- Have I encouraged the spread of scandal?
- Am I guilty of any type of fraud?
- Did I insult or tease others with the intention of hurting them?
- Have I falsely flattered others?
- Have I made rash judgments about others?
- Did I fail to keep secret what should be confidential?

OTHER SINS
- Have I intentionally refused to mention some grave sin in my previous confessions?
- Have I fulfilled my obligation to go to confession at least once a year and to go worthily to Holy Communion at least during the Easter season?
- Have I fasted on Ash Wednesday and Good Friday?
- Have I abstained from meat on the Fridays of Lent and Ash Wednesday?

APPENDIX THREE

The Virtues

Answers from Session Four (p. 67):

Prudence—discernment; carefully choosing what is good, and the right way to obtain that good (see *CCC* 1806).

Justice—fairness; respecting the rights of others and the desire to give them what is right (see *CCC* 1807).

Fortitude—inner strength; the will to persevere in difficulties, in pursuit of what is good (see *CCC* 1808).

Temperance—moderation; the desire to balance the use of created goods, choosing justice for all over the desire for personal pleasure (see *CCC* 1809).

Other human virtues that are related to these "hinge" or cardinal virtues might include mercy (compassion), forgiveness (reconciliation), humility, generosity, charity, kindness, and industry. The *Catechism* also covers the theological virtues of faith, hope, and charity (see *CCC* 1812–1829) and lists joy, peace, and mercy as the "fruits" of charity (*CCC* 1829).

The gifts and fruits of the Holy Spirit are also essential to the Christian life. The *Catechism* says that the gifts of the Holy Spirit are "permanent dispositions which make man docile in following the promptings of the Holy Spirit" (*CCC* 1830). The gifts of the Holy Spirit are "wisdom, understanding, counsel, fortitude, knowledge, piety, and fear of the Lord" (*CCC* 1831). The fruits of the Holy Spirit, on the other hand, are "perfections that the Holy Spirit forms in us as the first fruits of eternal glory. The tradition of the Church lists twelve of them: 'charity, joy, peace, patience, kindness, goodness, generosity, gentleness, faithfulness, modesty, self-control, chastity'" (*CCC* 1832).

"Renewing Truths"

Each session includes a "Renewing Truth" that you should focus on that week. They are reprinted here so that you may cut them out and place them on a mirror, car visor, or other place where you are likely to see them and be reminded to put the week's truth into practice.

"RENEWING TRUTH": *Session One*
Each time I look in the mirror I will say:
"I am intentionally and uniquely made for a relationship with God, who says, 'You are precious in my eyes, and honored, and I love you' "
(Isaiah 43:4).

"RENEWING TRUTH": *Session Two*
Each time I eat food, I will remind myself:
"I am what I eat. Fill me with you, Lord, even as 'the disciples were filled with joy and with the Holy Spirit'" (Acts 13:52).

"RENEWING TRUTH": *Session Three*
Every time I put on my clothes or coat, I will remind myself that you wrap me in your love, you are safe, and you are transforming me by your love every minute of each new day. I will say,
"He must decrease, but I must increase" (John 3:30).

"Renewing Truth": *Session Four*

Every time I must wait in line, on hold, in traffic, or for the microwave to ding, or when someone is standing on my last nerve, I will say, "I am growing in virtue. Jesus, I trust in you." To help me remember, I will tape this verse in a place where I will see it often:

> Trust in the Lord with all your heart,
> and do not rely on your own insight.
> In all your ways acknowledge him,
> and he will make straight your paths (Proverbs 3:5–6).

"Renewing Truth": *Session Five*

Every time I go in or out of my door I will say,
"I praise you, God, for _____. Your Word says, 'The joy of the Lord is [my] strength'!" (Nehemiah 8:10).

"Renewing Truth": *Session Six*

Every time I do [the laundry, the dishes, something I don't really like doing], I will do it humbly and say yes, offering it up as an act of love for God and allowing him to transform it into a "reproductive" act. I will repeat in my mind:

> "Love is patient; love is kind.… It bears all things, believes all things,
> hopes all things, endures all things"
> (1 Corinthians 13:4, 7).

NOTES

1. John of the Cross, *The Collected Works of St. John of the Cross,* Kieran Kavanaugh, and Otilio Rodriguez, ed. and trans. (Washington, DC: ICS, 1991), 53.

2. *Diary of Saint Maria Faustina Kowalska: Divine Mercy in My Soul* (Stockbridge, MA: Marian Helpers, 1987), entry 1264, p. 456.

3. John of the Cross, 52.

4. Jacques Philippe, *Interior Freedom* (New York: Scepter, 2007), 42.

5. Philippe, 86–87.

6. Teresa of Avila, "Sixth Mansion," in *Interior Castle,* E. Allison Peers, ed. and trans. (New York: Image, 1989), 194.

7. John of the Cross, 52.

8. John of the Cross, 76.

9. The word *pneuma* (πνεῦμα), pronounced NOO-mah, is used for all these words in the Bible: breath, wind, and spirit.

10. John of the Cross, 80.

11. John of the Cross, 80.

12. Daily readings can be found online through www.magnificat.com, the Laudate app, and www.usccb.org.

13. See http://www.usccb.org/prayer-and-worship/sacraments-and-sacramentals/penance/examinations-of-conscience.cfm or http://www.thelightisonforyou.org/confession/#examen.

14. These materials have been adapted from USCCB materials and the diocese of Fall River's "Be Reconciled to God" Initiative, available at http://www.bereconciledtogod.com/pdfs/examinationofconscience2010.pdf.

RECOMMENDED READING

ST. JOHN OF THE CROSS

Dubay, Thomas. *Fire Within: St. Teresa of Avila, St. John of the Cross, and the Gospel, on Prayer*. San Francisco: Ignatius, 1989.

John of the Cross. *The Collected Works of St. John of the Cross*. Washington, DC: Institute of Carmelite Studies, 1979.

Stinissen, Wilfried. *Into Your Hands, Father: Abandoning Ourselves to the God Who Loves Us*. San Francisco: Ignatius, 2011.

PRAYER

Foster, Richard J. *Celebration of Discipline: The Path to Spiritual Growth*. San Francisco: Harper & Row, 1988.

BUTTERFLY RESEARCH

Howse, P.E. *Seeing Butterflies: New Perspectives on Colour, Pattern & Mimicry*. Berkshire, UK: Papadakis, 2014.

Klots, Alexander B. *Eastern Butterflies: Peterson Field Guides*. New York: Mifflin, 1979.

Leach, William. *Butterfly People: An American Encounter with the Beauty of the World*. New York: Pantheon, 2013.

Nijhout, H. Frederik. *The Development and Evolution of Butterfly Wing Patterns*. Washington, DC: Smithsonian Institution, 1991.

Oberhauser, Karen Suzanne, and Michelle J. Solensky. *Monarch Butterfly Biology & Conservation*. Ithaca, NY: Cornell University Press, 2004.

Pyle, Robert Michael, and Lincoln P. Brower. *Chasing Monarchs Migrating with the Butterflies of Passage*. New Haven, CT: Yale University Press, 2014.

WEB

http://www.ncbi.nlm.nih.gov/pmc/articles/PMC2929297/

http://www.monarchwatch.org/index.html

https://www.learner.org/jnorth/monarch/

http://monarchlab.org/biology-and-research/
biology-and-natural-history/breeding-life-cycle/life-cycle/

http://www.thebutterflysite.com/life-cycle.shtml

https://askabiologist.asu.edu/monarch-life-cycle

WAYS TO GET INVOLVED TO HELP TO SAVE THE MONARCH

http://www.monarchwatch.org

http://www.saveourmonarchs.org

http://www.xerces.org

CHRISTIAN ENVIRONMENTAL GROUPS

http://christianteens.about.com/od/christianliving/tp/8-Christian-
Environmental Organizations.htm

GET READY TO SOAR!

If you're looking to spread your wings, this journal is just the beginning! Author Melissa Overmyer is ready to walk you through your spiritual journey from tiny egg to radiant butterfly in the *Born to Soar* online course. This six-week series offers prayers, reflections, and inspiring discussion of God's transformative love.

Go to franciscanmedia.org/soar to register, and use the discount code PLEXIPPUS to access the full course (a $30 value) for free!

Made in the USA
San Bernardino, CA
25 June 2017